The Impressionists

The Impressionists

Leon Amiel
Editor

Leon Amiel Publisher
New York

Published by
LEON AMIEL PUBLISHER
NEW YORK

© 1985 by Leon Amiel Publisher, Inc.

ISBN 0-8148-0739-9

Printed in the United States of America

Table of Contents

Introduction

Nothing seems easier at first sight than defining Impressionism. Since the movement is well-known, it would seem to be enough to name the painters who were associated with it and to define the characteristics of their works. But when one pays close attention to the distinctive traits of each painter, one quickly realizes that in certain areas there are many more contrasts than similarities.

Some impressionist painters, for example, can be defined as working in an orthodox manner (especially Monet, Pissarro, Sisley). There are others for whom Impressionism served only as a stimulus, a friendly environment, a shortlived temptation, a stage in their development or a starting point. It is important, when all of these artists are brought together under the title of Impressionism, not to lose sight of these differences. Of course it would be wrong to try to deprive the movement of its real significance, but at the same time the personal contribution of the main artists related to it must be emphasized. The more one studies their pictures, the more one realizes that they are each the unique expression of powerful and original personalities.

This observation is the guiding idea of this book. Obviously there is not enough space here to consider all the painters who may have been linked in one way or another with Impressionism. The criterion for selection has always been the importance and scope of the paintings, regardless of whether the artists were highly representative of the tendency, were simply close to it, influenced by it, or whether they borrowed some elements from it. This book intends to show that the Impressionist period is a great one that not only inaugurated a new art but enriched us with a long and splendid series of masterworks.

Burning of the Houses of Parliament.

Joseph Mallord William Turner

Maiden Lane (Covent Garden), London, April 23, 1775 — London, December 19, 1851.

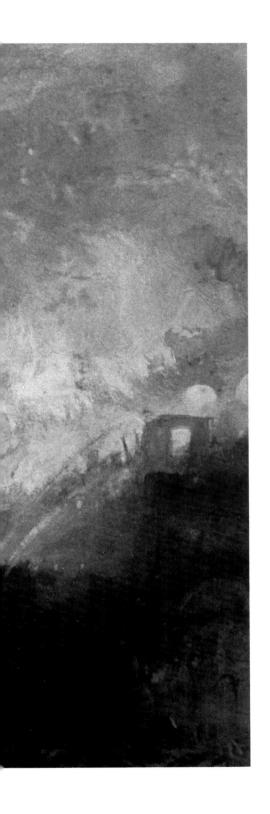

His canvases with mauves, artificial greens, blacks, and whites identify him as a subtle colorist but above all he was able to draw boldly and incisively, displaying both freedom and precision as he recreated forms with deft strokes.

The Fall of the Avalanche.

The Fighting Temeraire.

Alba at Norham Castle.

Rain, Steam, and Speed. ➜

It is possible to affirm that before Impressionism, Turner was already its spokesman, with his visionary gift for creating an enchanting transposition of reality by means of light and colors.

After being trained by Thomas Girtin, who was two years older and was the most outstanding member of the English school of watercolorists, Turner, in imitation of Claude Lorrain's *Liber veritatis*, began a *Liber studiorum*, consisting of a series of mezzotint (half-color) engravings which he continued for more than twelve years (there are sixty plates intended to accompany his drawings). For didactic purposes, he included observations and recollections of his travels in the Rhine Valley, in Italy (where he rejected an ineptly taught Classicism), Switzerland (where he completed many sketches at Valais), and Savoy (he painted the *Mer de Glace* at Chamonix).

Nevertheless, Turner's talents fully burst forth as a form of Impressionism before its time during the periods between 1830 and 1837 when he stayed at Petworth House in Sussex as a guest of Lord Egremont whom he accompanied on repeated jaunts to places of debauchery.

At Petworth which was the principal residence of his friend and patron, Turner created oil paintings and gouaches characterized by a sense of freedom where descriptive intentions were discarded, so that he could evoke the imagined qualities of salons where recollections of pianos, or sofas, or wandering pets, or the images of ghost-like figures confined by doors or mirrors, mingle pell-mell beneath bursts of light glimmering with unexpectedly subtle hues. Turner also developed a distinctly imprecise way of depicting vast expanses of water, or horizons dappled with different golden and silvery hues.

11

His *Rain, Steam, and Speed* (1844) at the National Gallery in London, where a locomotive is shown hurtling along a viaduct at full speed, is undoubtedly the painting which most closely resembles an Impressionist masterpiece, even though Turner completed this painting thirty years before the exhibition which would ultimately provide a name for the new movement. Turner had succeeded in introducing Time in painting.

Through Turner, it is possible to gain a fuller understanding of the possibilities and limits which French Impressionism would encounter: an unexpected mingling of naturalist reality with free and imaginative brushstrokes. For Monet and Pissarro, dreams, poetry, and imagination would spring from a bell-tower at Veteuil, from the banks of the Seine at Argenteuil, or from a marketplace in Pontoise (as Constable and Courbet would have done, these painters continued to select definite sites and themes), but, in Turner's paintings, every element, contrary to appearances, melts into "a fantasy inundated with light," or "a dense pink and blue mist," while "a pale firmament recedes into oblivion, disappearing within a mother-of-pearl horizon, reverberating and flowing within glistening water" (Huysmans). The author of *Certains* also referred to "these bursts of clarity" and these "torrents of daylight refracted through milky clouds dappled with fiery reds and streaked with violet, like the priceless center of an opal."

Turner possessed a footloose spirit, and he enjoyed creating an air of mystery. Although he was extremely successful and even somewhat miserly, he was a heavy drinker who was not interested in fame. Thus, he turned his back upon mundane concerns in order to escape from bothersome visitors. He often remained away from his home without anyone's knowing his whereabouts. Toward the end of his life, his housekeeper, Mrs. Danby, became concerned during one of his protracted absences and embarked upon an effort to find him. Turner had strayed to a small house near the Battersea Bridge, where he was living under the name of "Mr. Booth" and was posing as a retired sailor. He customarily went to the pubs, to drink with sailors, where he spoke like an expert about life at sea, shipwrecks, and flotillas lost among the vast,

San Benedetto, Venice.

The Houses of Parliament on Fire.

crashing waves which he had depicted, full of majesty, terror, and infiniteness. Finally, he was taken back to his home on Queen Anne Street, where he died.

Today, Turner's true merits are to be found in works which, during his lifetime, could not be exhibited. More than any other painter, Turner was capable of imagining colors (we know that he had read Goethe's *Farbenlehre*). One of Turner's biographers, P. G. Hamerton, has written: "There was never an artist who studied his predecessors so assiduously before displaying so much independence thereafter." Ruskin, in attempting to render Turner's works comprehensible, wrote that "if one allows the eye to follow an object disappearing into the distance, it gradually loses its impact, its distinctness, it structural composition, and all of its comprehensible qualities, but it *never* loses its gradations of light."

Sunset on the Sea.

 *Mer de Glace, Chamonix, con la capanna di Blair.*

 *Sea Funeral.*

Landscape with Windmill.

Johann Barthold Jongkind

Lattrop (Holland), June 3, 1819 — Asile Saint-Rambert (near Grenoble), January 27, 1891.

He had a talent for only painting the essential and for concentrating his attention upon the principal locations where colors and light were visible, with a unique gift for accentuating them.

Gate at Monceau.

Vue de Paris, la Seine.

Entrance to the Port of Honfleur.

This Dutchman was a highly original artist who heralded the future. He suffered from periods of inactivity, combined with a persecution complex attributed to abuse of absinthe. His strong-willed wife, Mme. Fesser, played the role of a guardian angel who obliged him to leave Paris and settle near Grenoble at La Côte-Saint-André.

As a direct precursor of the Impressionists, Jongkind was an unusual painter who adopted the role of a somewhat crude and rather primitive artist. In order to achieve a more original mode of expression, he expanded upon concepts which he had acquired from his mentor, Isabey, who aided him and regarded him as a disciple.

Jongkind initially adopted the customary style of Dutch painting, namely the style of Van der Neer and the skaters at Averkamp, before beginning to use his brush more freely, performing rapid movements typical of sketches and watercolors. He occasionally resided in Honfleur and frequently visited the farm of Saint-Simeon, owned by Toutain, where he met Boudin, Courbet and Baudelaire. Anticipating Utrillo, he painted street scenes, with advertising placards appearing in bold print on walls and in shop windows.

Jongkind had a talent for only painting the essential and for concentrating his attention upon the principal locations where colors and light were visible, with a unique gift for accentuating them, as can be observed in his *Vue de Paris* (Paris Scene), where Nôtre Dame appears in the distance (1863).

His cerebral malady grew worse at the height of his success, and he was taken to the Asile Saint-Rambert near Grenoble where he died at the age of sixty-two.

The Beach of Sainte-Adresse.

Fishing Boats.

Le Havre.

The Skaters.

23

Demolition, Rue des Francs-Bourgeois.

Les Bateaux au large de scapa flow.   *Rue Saint-Jacques in Paris.* ➔

A Bar at the Folies-Bergère.

Edouard Manet

French painter, Paris, 1823-1883.

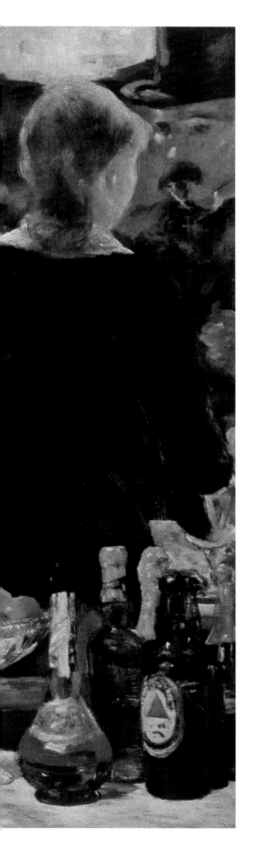

The natural elegance of his work permitted him to be a precise and exact observer, who never fell into the slightest vulgarity.

← *Lola de Valence.*

The Dead Toreador.

Manet belonged to the upper middle class, and his existence was bound to that class; he remained attached to the privileges it enjoys, wished to receive the honors and recognition it confers, and at the same time gave rise during his lifetime to the most violent scandals and unwittingly produced through his painting a complete revolution.

He brought a taste for liberty that corresponded to the aspirations of the time but had not yet been admitted in its consequences. Academic art was still dominated by what was thought to be a tradition but in fact consisted of no more than the impoverished remnants of superannuated formulae. At the beginning Manet probably had no intention of playing the part of a revolutionary leader. He had very prudently begun by setting out upon a more conventional career. Yielding to family insistence, he started out in 1848 as a student pilot on a training ship, and made the voyage to South America. When he returned, he failed his examination at the Naval School and at last succeeded in persuading his father to let him become a painter.

In January 1850, he joined the studio of Thomas Couture. His independence brought him into immediate conflict with his teacher. He did not, however, approach the profession with preconceived ideas, sure of inventing a personal technique. He frequented the Louvre very as-

siduously, his lessons left him unsatisfied, and the example of masterpieces convinced him that he had more to learn from the masters and from Nature.

His character as a painter therefore derived from his stays in Fontainebleau and from his admiration of Tintoretto, Titian and Velasquez. In his first works, already stamped by these influences, an inclination can be discerned for clear colors, a free touch, and large, vibrant flat areas. His visits to Holland, Germany and Italy reinforced this tendency, in which he was reviving the freedom and dash of Frans Hals and the Venetians of the Renaissance. His *Portrait of a Spanish Musician* won an "honorable mention" at the Salon of 1861 and, because of the subject, also earned the praises of Théophile Gautier.

The following year, a show given by a troupe of Spanish singers and dancers made him all the more enthusiastic about Spain and inspired a whole series of paintings. The famous *Lola of Valencia*, which Baudelaire called a "jewel in pink and black," was one of them. The affinities between Manet's art and Spanish painting were once thought so obvious that a critic described Manet as a "Parisian Spaniard," and Courbet, on the occasion of the 1865 Salon, where *Olympia* was exhibited, said: "This young fellow had better not try to pull Velasquez over our eyes." However, it was not until that year that Manet finally went to Spain to see the masters by whom he was

29

Luncheon on the Grass.

supposed to have been influenced. His admiration for Velasquez was strengthened and he discovered Goya.

From the beginning, then, Manet was astonishing and bewildering. The first violent reactions of the public occurred in 1863 when he exhibited *Le Déjeuner sur l'Herbe* at the famous *Salon des Refusés.* The scandals attributed to this picture are difficult to understand today. However, it seemed indecent because it represented a naked woman sitting on the grass between some young men in contemporary dress.

At the time nudes were tolerated only in allegorical scenes when the figures were supposed to represent gods. Actually it is very likely that the technique was even more shocking than the subject. With its freshness and vivacity of color and its broad execution, the canvas seemed to have been painted on the very spot rather than in the studio. All this indicated on the part of the young artist an inexcusably warped character, an audacity which made him exceed the limits of decency. The rejection of convention, the boldness of the elements employed had at the time an aggressive character, which, in drawing the opprobrium of the righteous bourgeoisie down upon him, made Manet the leader of the young painters.

His attitude became even more apparent at the Salon of 1865, where he exhibited *Olympia.* Zola found it the pictorial counterpart of the theories he was himself beginning to elaborate. He felt in the work, in its reaction against accepted standards, a frankness and certainty revealing an art already liberated and sure of itself, leaving all hesitations and gropings behind it. The public was offended by the presence of a black cat at the foot of the bed, and the Negress offering a bouquet of flowers seemed out

The Fifer.

of place. The critics, for their part, deplored the lack of shading, the brutality of the drawing and the crudity of the light, which they did not go so far as to insult. Jules Claretie, very categorical in his denunciations, typified the attitude adopted by the antagonists: "What is this odalisque with the yellow belly, some indecent model picked up God knows where, presuming to represent Olympia? Olympia? What Olympia? A prostitute, beyond a doubt. E. Manet will never be reproached for idealizing the foolish virgins — he'll drag them all through the mud, more likely."

The model Claretie, so grossly insulted, was the pretty Victorine Meurend, the central figure of *Le Déjeuner sur l'Herbe* before she became *Olympia* and who was to be *The Fifer* the following year. Today, *Olympia* seems to us one of the finest achievements of modern art. In it one admires the unexpectedness of the pose, the firmness and purity of outline, the sincerity of the expression, and the consummate mastery of the composition. Enclosed in its abstract but still living whiteness, seldom has a woman's body known such nudity.

The painters a few years younger than Manet who were soon to create Impressionism did not underestimate the importance of these experiments. They recognized in Manet a precursor behind whom they could gather to renew painting more drastically than the art of a Courbet or a Corot had undertaken to do, much as they admired those painters. Manet benefited in turn from the good feel-

The Old Musician.

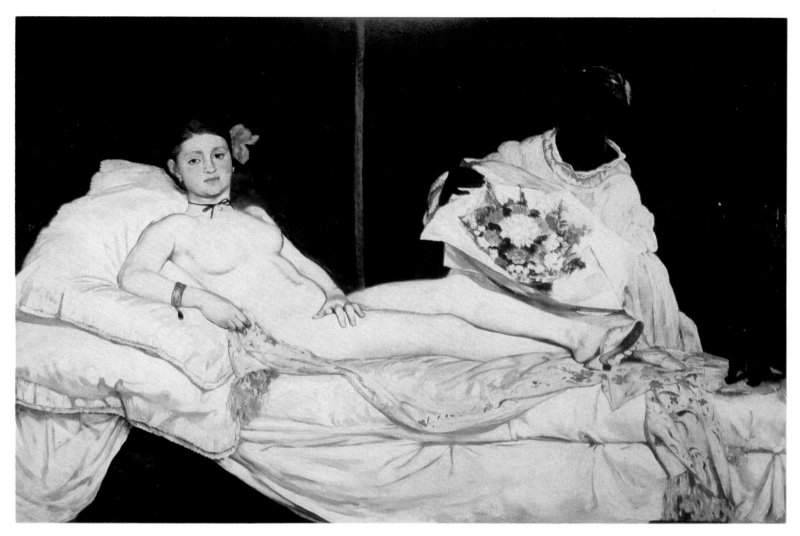

Olympia.

ing of the younger men; having set them the example of his mastery and youthful boldness, he found them, with their glorification of light color, a stimulus and a new source of inspiration.

Although he did not participate in the Impressionist exhibitions organized after 1874, he felt the appeal of this renovation, as his lightened palette testifies. However, he did not become devoted to landscape for his own sake; his outdoor scenes always contained figures, which were the occasion for him to arrange, among the blue and grey reflections with which he surrounded them, dark colors that were set off by the contrast. While he shared with the Impressionists the desire to express sense impressions in all their immediacy, he never resorted to the systematic breakdown of color.

Unlike his young friends, he had no horror of black — quite the opposite. Black was to him, as to Frans Hals, a real color, which he often used, and which gave an extraordinary brightness to many of his compositions. Neither was he haunted by plastic problems like Cézanne, or

obsessed with drawing like Degas. Manet did not attempt to set up a system; less a theoretician than a painter, instinctively inspired and gifted, he wanted, above all, to recreate on canvas the vividness and intensity of what he experienced. No doubt he was always surprised by the scorn he encountered in academic circles.

For a long time he persisted in exhibiting at the Salon and ended by being awarded a secondary medal that put him out of the running. But this was in 1881, and his career was already fulfilled — so much so, in fact, that the next year he was made Chevalier of the Legion of Honor (through the intervention of Antonin Proust, his fellow student at the Collège Rollin, who had by then become Minister of Fine Arts).

The art of Manet is an introduction to the future, in its freedom of handling and the importance accorded to color. Even when he applied the pigments flat and refused to tone them down, his color retained spatiality, and this was probably his most characteristic contribution to the art of his time.

Departure of the Folkestone Boat.

← *La Femme aux bocks.*

The Barricade.

At the Café.

The importance he gave to color made him sometimes summarize the surface of a volume in a few essential planes and sometimes, on the contrary, adopt broad, uniformly colored surfaces, as in *The Fifer*. It was in connection with this canvas that Daumier accused him of wanting to reduce the painting to the "faces on playing cards." This was a failure to recognize the boldness of Manet's experiment; for thus to plant a figure in vivid and brilliantly colored dress against the emptiness of a monochrome background suggested by Velasquez without allowing such extreme simplification to end in a total lack of life, called for the very surest kind of hand. Although every shadow has disappeared and become concentrated in the vibrancy of outline round the form, it is astonishing that this mysterious process has not allowed either the fluidity of outline or solidity of form to diminish.

The art of Manet, in spite of all innovations in technique, is nevertheless bound to tradition, because of the influences it has felt, and especially because of the overall concept of a picture that it presupposes. Like the very great artists, Manet was able to take a hackneyed theme and give it such life that it seemed new. Without proof, an unsuspecting person would not think of Rubens behind *Le Déjeuner sur l'Herbe* or Titian behind *Olympia*, and yet the relationship is indisputable. *Le Pêche* (*Fishing*) mixes elements found in two works of Rubens: *The Rainbow* and *The Park of The Castle of Steen*; also from Rubens comes *The Nymph Surprised*, a reversed fragment from *Susanna at the Bath. The Dead Toreador* is a replica of *The Dead Warrior* of Velasquez, and *The Execution of Maximilian*, a pendant to Goya's *The Second of May*. These are neither imitations nor plagiarisms, but real creations starting from an external and independent reality, whether it be an object, a person, or another picture.

No matter what theme he selected, Manet fits it to the measure of his own personality. There is no less intensity or life in the canvases inspired by classic works than there is in *The Bar at the Folies-Bergère*, the subject of which was taken from an episode in contemporary life; and this composition conforms to laws no less severe than the others do. Throughout all his changes Manet preserved a surprising unity. No doubt the ability of some men to invent a new vision, so unexpected that it comes as a surprise, and yet so perfectly in accord with still unformulated aspirations, that its style immediately compels recognition, is a sign of genius. Works like these are of lasting value; when they can no longer surprise they become classics, for the feeling of life they diffuse bears witness to their truth.

Free as it may seem, the art of Manet is not improvised; his compositions are not the product of chance but are rigorously and purposefully constructed. He is not so entirely

Mademoiselle Victorine in the Costume of an Espada. ➡

The Band in the Tuileries Gardens.

Argenteuil. ➤

detached from the subject as might be believed, at least not so detached as his successors. He was easily tempted by large historical compositions, not only in his youth, as the works discussed above reveal, but also when he was in complete control of his powers: *The Execution of Maximilian* furnishes an example. In 1879 he even proposed to the Prefect of the Seine to decorate the Hôtel de Ville with compositions depicting Paris life: the markets, the railways, the bridges and the race-track. Finally, in 1881, he produced a picture on the escape of Henri de Rochefort from the Noumea penitentiary, which illustrated an event hardly seven years old. One can conclude that he did not have the reticence about anecdote, or even the distaste for it, that began with Impressionism, and was to become one of the principles of modern art.

The interest he took in human subjects made him one of the best portraitists of the nineteenth century. The numerous portraits he did of Berthe Morisot, particularly

the one with the black hat, and those of Proust, Clemenceau, Théodore Duret, Zola, Irma Brunner and Méry Laurent, not to mention one of the finest, that of Stéphane Mallarmé, should not be forgotten.

Towards the end of his life, when he began to feel the onset of paralysis, he took up pastels, easier to handle, and produced portraits of Parisian celebrities that are among his finest accomplishments. The natural elegance of his work permitted him to be a precise and exact observer, who never fell into the slightest vulgarity. Although he always remained on the fringe of the Impressionist group and did not give up work in his studio for outdoor painting, as later artists did, Manet deserves the position of leader that is usually granted him in the history of Impressionism, for he was the first, and for years the only, painter to fight for a new art that sought a renewal of inspiration and technique in direct observation of Nature and contemporary life.

The Bridge at Villeneuve-la-Garenne.

Alfred Sisley

French painter, Paris, 1839 — Moret, 1899.

His delicate and tender art enabled him to evoke with infinite poetry and grace the peaceful and picturesque life.

Bridge at Hampton Court.

Together with Monet, Sisley represents Impressionism in its purest form. He was tempted less than anyone by portraits or still-lifes, except at the beginning; he confined himself almost exclusively to landscape, and his work did not undergo any profound change during the course of his life. His first known pictures, notably those he sent to the 1866 Salon, have been compared, in tonality, to the work of Corot and Courbet; this similarity revealed the nature of his preferences.

He was lucky enough not to experience materially difficult beginnings like his Impressionist friends, but when he began to fight for the new painting, he was ruined and felt financial hardship even more than they. While in their worst days Pissarro and Cézanne received forty francs for their pictures, Sisley had more than once to give his away for thirty or even twenty-five. Moreover, he died before he could benefit from the triumph of his ideas and his work. Immediately after his death his talent was recognized and his paintings soon fetched high prices.

Sisley's art consists almost entirely of landscapes, and even for these he confined himself to the valley of the Seine, the Ile-de-France, especially the Fontainebleau region, of which he remains one of the most authentic interpreters. He succeeded admirably, and with as much sensibility as Monet, in transcribing the movement of foliage or the scintillation of light on water; but at the same time he succeeded better than Monet in preserving the structure of the landscape by not reducing it to luminous effects with unstable colors.

Form remained firm in his work, not dissolved in the atmosphere; a tree is a tree, a house a house. There is nothing systematic in his art. He did not adopt the low horizons of Boudin, and while he gave an important place to the sky in certain pictures, this was because, in its movement and color, it was part of the subject he was representing. In each of his canvases he gives the impression of having achieved as much as possible. One could not imagine thicker undergrowth than the ones he painted in the

Women Going to the Woods.

Louveciennes Hill-tops at Marly.

The Regattas.

Boats on the Seine.

La Route de St. Germain à Marly.

Landscape of Louveciennes.

forest of Fontainebleau, scenes of floods more desperate than those he transcribed at Port-Marly, snow scenes more sadly luminous than those of Louveciennes, springtimes clearer than those at Saint-Mammès, although he avoided dramatizing his subjects.

His delicate and tender art enabled him to evoke with infinite poetry and grace the peaceful and picturesque life of the town of Moret, where he lived permanently after 1879. Although he experienced a fate similar to that of the other Impressionists, although he had also attended courses at the Atelier Gleyre in his youth, like Bazille, Monet and Renoir, and had fallen back upon the modest

generosity of the baker and collecter Murer, little has been written about his work and life. This is not because he lacked talent, but rather because his life was neither adventurous nor picturesque, because his art was entirely ruled by sensibility, did not strive to illustrate a rigorously established system and thus does not lend itself to commentary.

Neither a few sojourns in England, his wish to be received at the Salon nor poverty shook Sisley's conviction or altered his art. As modest in his ambitions as he was tenacious in his convictions, he remained true to himself and to his friends.

Flood of Port Marly.

Lordship Lane Station, Upper Norwood.

Camille Pissarro

Painter, Saint-Thomas in the West Indies, 1830 — Paris, 1903.

The artist was attracted by golden and silver effects, vast stretches of green, delicate foliage, streams and mottled skies — the principal element in his picture became Light itself.

L'Hermitage, Pontoise.

The Crossroads, Pontoise,

"Of all painters," says Cézanne, "Pissarro was nearest to Nature." His entire life was devoted to observing the changing effects of Nature, which he succeeded in capturing in innumerable oil paintings, water-colors, drawings and engravings. He never tired of studying the same village church, the same fields in different seasons, a market place, the Paris boulevards, and he infused a rare poetic quality into these subjects.

He had a long struggle with his parents — a French father and a Creole mother — before obtaining their consent to leave the West Indies to study art in Paris, and had reached the age of twenty-five when finally he arrived in France. His first enthusiasm was for Corot, and he started work under his supervision, with permission to style himself "pupil of Corot." But his aged tutor disapproved when in 1865 Pissarro joined up with Monet, Renoir and other young artists grouped around Manet, though Daubigny and Courbet (whose influence is evident in some of Pissarro's early work) accepted the newcomers with goodwill.

In 1870 Monet and Pissarro fled to London to escape the Prussian occupation, and there found Daubigny who gave them valuable help and advice and introduced them to the young French art dealer Durand-Ruel, whose name has since become firmly linked with that of the Impressionists. Durand-Ruel bought Pissarro's work first in London and then on a larger scale in Paris; little by little he became the regular dealer of Monet, Pissarro and all their friends, sharing their setbacks as well as their painfully slow climb to fame.

In England Pissarro studied Turner and Constable. On his return to France he found his house looted and his canvases (nearly a thousand) destroyed. But his joy at being back in France lent him courage, and he settled in Pontoise, where Cézanne came to work with him (1872-1874) and profit from his advice. Pissarro made regular trips to Paris, thus keeping in touch with his friends.

With them, in 1874, he countered the official Salon's systematic refusal to hang their work by organizing the first independent picture exhibition. A hostile critic writing about this exhibition, in the *Charivari* of April 25th, first applied the word "Impressionists" to their work. The following eight exhibitions organized by the Impressionists between 1874 and 1886, which met mainly with ridicule and insults, were due in large part to Pissarro's indefatigable initiative and his gift for reconciling adverse factions. He was the only member of the group to exhibit at each show, and he was alone in offering his friendship to the younger painters of promise.

Peasants and Haystack.

La Côte des Boeufs à Pontoise.

Entry to the Village of Voisins.

Paris, Boulevard Montmartre at Night.

Two Young Peasant Women.

In 1879 he interested himself in Gauguin and introduced him to the group. Later he joined up with Seurat and Signac in their efforts to reconcile art with science, and he insisted on their being included in the final exhibition of 1886.

Pissarro, senior by two years to Manet and by ten to Monet, was the eldest of the group. Without exception, all the painters and writers included in his circle felt a profound esteem for this kind and gentle man, who united an innate goodness with an indomitable fighting spirit. A convinced atheist, Pissarro was also a socialist tinged with anarchist ideas, and he considered the artistic struggle as inseparable from the question of the artist's role in modern society. But however radical his views, they were free from

hate and imbued with a disinterested integrity which commanded general respect even among those less socially conscious than he. Everyone knew of his personal difficulties, his continual fight to provide for his family of six children, and they could not but admire the composure and complete lack of bitterness with which he discussed the essential artistic or political problems of his day.

Pissarro never ceased to advocate humility before Nature, though he refrained from imposing his ideas on others. The advice he gave to Cézanne and Gauguin must have been similar to that given to his children, to whom he wrote in one of his admirable letters: "Beware of trusting to my judgment! I am so anxious to see you succeed that

Jallais Hill, Pontoise.

I don't hide my opinions from you; but only accept what corresponds to your own feeling and way of understanding. What I most fear is that you should resemble me too much. So go ahead, and work!" To this respect for the individual he added a rare gift for pedagogy. "He was so wonderful a teacher," said Mary Cassatt, "that he could have taught a stone to draw correctly."

Pissarro's artistic development can be divided into various phases. His early work shows the influence of Corot and Courbet; a poetic conception of Nature is expressed in hardy strokes of the palette knife and his colors are often as dramatically somber as those in Cézanne's first paintings. Little by little his colors grew lighter and he stressed the solidity of masses in subtle but opaque shades, greys often dominating.

"As early as 1865," Cézanne tells us, "he eliminated black, bistre, sienna browns and ochres." It was just before the 1870 war that he took the decisive step towards light coloring and the analysis of shadow, and the study of English landscape painters during his exile in London encouraged him to pursue this course and confirmed his conclusions. The outcome was the series of intensely vital, lyrical canvases painted between 1870 and 1880 — his truly "Impressionist" period of open-air painting and discoveries in the use of color.

Light itself became a "subject" — the principal element in his picture. The artist was attracted by golden and silver

Paysage au Valhermeil.

effects, vast stretches of green, delicate foliage, trees in
flower, corn-fields, streams and mottled skies. He studied
all these first around Pontoise, then at Osny and Éragny-
sur-Epte near Gisors, where he settled in 1885. With these
lighter colors he worked in small comma-like brush
strokes, which enabled him to depict the brilliance of light
without breaking up the forms on which it shone.

By 1884 Pissarro began to feel dissatisfaction with this
technique, finding it too crude, and it is not surprising to
find him attracted in the following years to Divisionism
(*vide* Neo-Impressionism) in an attempt to reconcile
Seurat's rigid theories with his own poetic temperament.
This effort was doomed to failure; in 1890 Pissarro began
to realize, as he put it, "the impossibility of following my
sensations, and consequently of expressing life and movement and rendering Nature's marvelous but fugitive efforts, of giving individuality to my drawings;" so he aban-

Blvd. Montmartre, Winter Morn.

doned the Pointillist technique "to retrieve with difficulty and by hard work what I had lost, without losing whatever I may have found."

Pissarro spent the last years of his life in the search for a new liberty of expression. His efforts were astonishingly fruitful and in his view of Rouen and Paris he succeeded in uniting exquisite sensibility with a superbly vigorous technique. Profiting from his Impressionist and Divisionist experiments, his art became powerful yet subtle, firm of line and rich in coloring. Though mainly a landscape artist, Pissarro also painted portraits, still-lifes and nudes. "If we examine Pissarro's art as a whole," wrote Gauguin in 1902, "in spite of a certain unevenness, we find not only a tremendous artistic will which is never belied, but also an essentially intuitive, pure-bred art. He took from everyone, you say? Why not? Everyone, though denying him, took from him too."

Max Schmidt in a Single Scull.

Thomas Eakins

American painter, sculptor and teacher, Philadelphia, 1844-1916.

He achieved an art more consummate in penetrating observation and plastic pictorial space than any other contemporary American master.

The Pain-Oared Shell.

The finest American painter of his time. Eakens spent six years studying art at the Pennsylvania Academy of Fine Arts. He also studied anatomy—a field in which he became as proficient as any physician of the day—at the Jefferson Medical College in Philadelphia. At the age of 22, he visited Paris for a period of studies at the École des Beaux-Arts from 1866-1869 and studied under Jean-Léon Gerome Augustin Dumont, and León Bonnat. It has not been generally recognized that it was from these French Academicians that Eakens absorbed much of his love for meticulous handling and objective realism, the structure of forms, and even certain themes—such as his later boating scenes of the 1870's.

Upon visiting Spain in December, 1869, however, Eakens immediately found inspiration in the dark, muted palettes and penetrating realism of Diego Velasquez (1599-1660), and Jasepe de Ribera (1591-1652). The art of these Spanish masters, along with the precepts of the French Academicians under whom he studied, profoundly influenced his painting.

Eakens returned to America in July 1870, settled at 1729 Mount Vernon Street, Philadelphia, and never again left his native land. More than any other master of such lofty stature, his art became intimately associated with the close community around his home. He began to paint the everyday life of his friends and associates in the Philadelphia area as well as outdoor sporting events and portraits in a completely realistic style. Prominant among his early works are rowing scenes and portraits that display a probing and precise vision, a tight sense of structure, and psychologically revealing rendering of the human subject. The rigorous clarity of these paintings such as *John Biglen in a Single Scull* (1874), Yale University Art Gallery, New Haven, is emphasized by the total mastery of anatomy and the calculating evocation of outdoor light. The light reveals and clarifies form and does not dissolve it as it does in works by the European Impressionists.

As a result of his familiarity with the staff of the Jefferson Medical College, Eakens painted the finest work of his early period and one of the towering achievements of American art, *The Gross Clinic* (1875, Jefferson Medical College). This huge painting portrayed the eminent surgeon, Samuel D. Gross, in the midst of an operation before a class of his students. The uncompromising realism displayed by the bloodstained hand of the doctor as well as the patient's pathetic, nakedly exposed, and bloody thigh, shocked the conservative sensibility of Eakens' contemporaries.

The impact of the medical realism still conjures up, after a lapse of almost 250 years, the equally arresting and similarly unmerciful medical realism achieved by Rembrandt in his *Anatomy Lesson of Dr. Tulp* (painted in 1632). In this Rembrandt painting, as in *The Gross Clinic*, a shaft of diagonal light illuminates a grisly passage of naked skin,

The Biglen Brothers' Regatta.

blood and bone and the head of a distinguished doctor who turns to instruct his subordinates. In Rembrandt and Eakens, the light which falls upon the faces of Dr. Tulp and Dr. Gross not only makes their heads the focal points of the two paintings but also serves as a kind of visual metaphor of the superior intellectual insight and learning possessed by the chief surgeon. As in many of his works, Eakens' signature in the *Gross Clinic* is placed upon a three dimensional object — the surgeon's operating table — rather than being placed haphazardly in a corner of the canvas.

The Gross Clinic has recently been described by one art critic as "the most powerful and important painting by a nineteenth century American artist, and certainly the most extraordinary historical painting by an American artist." This opinion was not shared by the critics of Eakens' time. The painting was rejected by the Centennial Exhibition art jury, but Eakens did succeed in having it hung in a corner in the Medical section of the Centennial Exhibition.

A fundamental tenet of Eakens' artistic credo was the use of scientific techniques, such as mathematics, to create a painting. And to his total command of anatomy, he added a pioneering expertise in photography as a means of capturing the human body in action. In 1884 he photographically recorded human and animal movement by using a single lense — an improvement over the technique of his associate Eadweard Muybridge who had been using a battery of cameras. With Eakens' single lense, the view-

point did not change and the time intervals between pictures could be exactly related in the manner of a motion picture. By using the camera to gather visual information, Eakens distilled such masterpieces of rhythmical anatomical movement as the *Swimming Hole* (1883). This work was produced with the aid of photographs taken by Eakens of the locale as well as of the nude male swimmers. It shows Eakens with a group of friends and students swimming in the nude at a secluded spot. The nudes, seen in various poses, recall the academic studies of the human body that Eakens had learned as a student at the École des Beaux Arts in Paris. In *The Swimming Hole*, Eakens disguises the academic influence by placing his nudes in an outdoor, rather than studio, setting.

As teacher at the Pennsylvania Art Academy, Eakens' method was founded upon painting from the nude. It is ironic therefore that among his finished paintings and from *The Swimming Hole*, there are very few nudes. The reason for this lay in his devotion to realism, his intention to render what he saw in the everyday life of his Philadelphia surroundings; and Philadelphians of the late nineteenth century had no tolerance for people who displayed themselves fully or even partially nude. Only in certain sporting events such as Eakens' beloved rowing or in prize fighting matches such as can be seen in *Between Rounds* (1899), could the musculature of male athletes be seen. Women were barred from taking part in such events.

John Biglen in Single Scull.

Biglen Brothers Turning the Stake Boat.

Often Eakens asked women sitting for their portraits whether they would pose in the nude for him. The scandals caused by such bold queries were second only to the uproar Eakens created at the Pennsylvania Art Academy when he insisted that his female students become experienced in drawing from nude male models. One day, in order to demonstrate the proper drawing of the male pelvis to his students, Eakens removed the loin cloth worn by the male model. Outraged and scandalized by such activities, a group of his female students reported him to the director of the Academy. After mounting pressure, Eakens resigned in 1886 from his teaching position, and with the aid of a group of disgruntled Academy students, helped found the Art Students League of Philadelphia.

The Art Students League was a cooperative art school, led by Eakens and run entirely by the students. Eakens did all the teaching and refused to take any salary. Lloyd Goodrich, in his well known monograph on Eakens, has perceptively seen that almost all Eakens' nudes, both female and male, are placed with their backs turned toward the spectator. Only at the very close of his career, in the 1908 *William Rush and His Model*, did Eakens

finally break with his former conventions by rendering a female nude seen from the front.

Eakens' interest in the Pennsylvania sculptor, William Rush reveals his struggle with the moral climate of the late 19th century. Rush had been commissioned in 1809 by the city of Philadelphia to carve an allegorical Grecian maiden in a clinging robe. In four versions of *William Rush and his Model* that Eakens painted, the posing model is rendered in the nude, even though Eakens was well aware that she probably never really posed in the nude for Rush. In the final 1908 version, Eakens himself appears in the guise of Rush, escorting the nude model down from the posing platform. Here Eakens was living out in his art a role that he all too seldom had a chance to play in real life.

After the middle of the 1880's, Eakens' art centered to an ever increasing degree upon portraits. Most of his sitters were either his friends or certain intellectuals who interested him by their work and their qualities of mind. Eakens often portrayed his sitters engaged in their work or surrounded, as is *Mrs. William D. Frishmuth* (1900; Philadelphia Museum of Art), by the objects they owned.

Miss Amelia Van Buren.

medical students of Dr. Agnew for 750 dollars. Once again Eakens took up the problems that he had mastered in the *Gross Clinic,* and now created a complex asymetrical composition in which the head of the chief surgeon is once more the focal point of a highly complex design. Again the vulnerable nakedness of the patient under the surgeon's knife was rendered, however this time in an even more merciless manner than he had done in the *Gross Clinic.* Taken together, both the *Gross Clinic* and the *Agnew Clinic* present the observer with the pitiful dilemma of man's naked helplessness in the face of illness, while at the same time the paintings celebrate the powers of the human mind in the battle against disease. When the observer turns away from these two paintings, the final visual impression that remains is not the vulnerable body under the scalpel, but rather the illuminated face of the surgeon, rapt in thought, and engrossed by the struggle for a successful cure.

The rejection of the *Agnew Clinic* by the Society of American Artists was the dismal evidence that the neglect of Eakens' art continued apace with his increasing mastery. He responded to this rejection with a letter to the Society that indicated his characteristic refusal to compromise either himself or his art:

> I desire to sever all connection with the Society of American Artists... For the last three years my paintings have been rejected by you, one of them the *Agnew Portrait,* a composition more important than any I have seen upon your walls...

An often overlooked aspect of Eakens' genius was his interest in sculpture. His few works in that medium were executed in a realist style which explored interests similar to those seen in his paintings. Among the finest examples of animal sculpture in American art are the two horses Eakens completed in 1891 for the bronze equestrian statues of Lincoln and Grant of the Memorial Arch at Prospect Park in Brooklyn. Eakens also completed (1892) two historical reliefs for the Trenton New Jersey Battle Monument.

It was not until the last decade of his life that he finally received a few of the awards and honors that should have come to him earlier. Unquestionably the most powerful master of figurative realism of his time in America, he achieved an art more consummate in penetrating observation and plastic pictorial space than any other contemporary American master. In his individuality and quality of his achievement he is rivalled in his own time and country perhaps only by Albert Pinkham Ryder — his antipode in almost every other respect.

Eakens' work is represented in the most important American collections, including The Metropolitan Museum of Art, the Philadelphia Museum of Art, and the Yale University Art Collection.

Mrs. Frishmuth, sits in the midst of her extensive collection of exotic musical instruments. She is portrayed as being deadened by her enforced idleness. Her social isolation has rendered her as superfluous to society as the old and odd instruments that surround her. Such portraits are a revelation of the plight of American women at the turn of the century. Eakens' men, such as *Henry A. Rowland* (1897; Addison Gallery of American Art) are often active as thinkers or involved in sporting events. Rowland was a professor of science. On the wooden frame that encloses the portrait of the seated Rowland, Eakens drew a decorative pattern of the mathematical formulas, measurements, and diagrams that had been the concerns of Rowland's career. The psychological insight of the late portraits place them among the best achievements of American art. Many of his sitters expected a flattering gloss of their features, and when, to their shock, they found their inner souls revealed, they refused to take away the finished work.

Another climax was reached in *The Agnew Clinic* (1889; University of Pennsylvania), commissioned by the

The Gross Clinic.

Crows Over the Wheatfield.

Vincent Van Gogh

Dutch painter, North Brabant, 1853 — Auvers-sur-Oise, 1890.

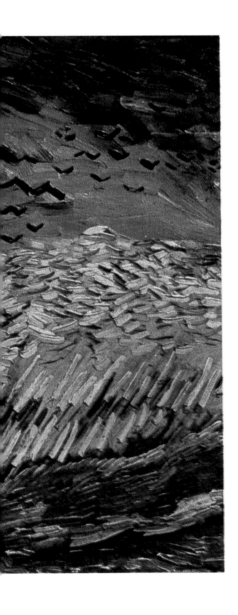

He wanted something peaceful and pleasant, realistic and yet painted with emotion ... full of calm and of pure harmony, comforting like music.

If, in December 1885, Van Gogh had not experienced a near-blinding revelation as a result of which he produced the masterpieces of the five last years of his life, he would no doubt be hailed today as a great painter of labor and poverty, of workmen and peasants overwhelmed by weariness, the first of the Dutch Expressionists. He became a painter in order to solve an inner conflict by which he was torn, to take his revenge in the domain of art for the failures he had experienced in his life.

He was of a Protestant family, a family of clergymen. But two of his uncles were art dealers, a fact that allowed him to start out in The Hague as a salesman in a gallery recently sold by one of them to the firm of Goupil of Paris. Vincent was sixteen then. Four years later, he was sent by his firm to London, to work in the English branch. In London he fell in love with his landlady's daughter. He asked her hand. He was turned down.

Unstable by temperament, acutely nervous, too sincere, he was deeply dejected by this first failure. He left London and went to work at Goupil's head office in Paris, in 1875. He was immediately borne away upon the current of ideas of which Paris was then the center. He read all the books within his reach, visited museums, underwent the influence of humanitarian writers and of painters concerned with the sufferings of the humble. The Bible became the chief stimulus of this self-taught son of a clergyman. He was dismissed by Goupil in 1876, and went back to England.

He worked at a small school at Ramsgate, and then at another, where he did some preaching. He applied for a job as an evangelist among the miners. "I feel drawn to religion. I want to comfort the humble." His application was rejected. At Christmas of the same year he returned to Etten, to his parents, but soon there was conflict. From January 21, to April 30, 1877, he was a clerk in a bookshop in Dordrecht. But he was unable to adjust himself to a practical and regular existence. Therefore, increasingly tormented by his religious calling, he went to Amsterdam to prepare for the entrance examination to the Theological College.

After fourteen months of desperately hard work, he had to give up and return to his family. His exasperated father entered him at the Evangelical school at Brussels.

In December 1878, Vincent left for the Borinage in Belgium without waiting to be given an appointment. He undertook to bring the miners of this forsaken region back to Christ. He adopted their own poverty, slept on a board in a wooden hut, shared their sufferings, attended the sick, showed the exalted zeal of an apostle, but without success. He was then an ill-clothed, gawky, red-haired fellow, with

← Sidewalk Café at Night.

Portrait of the Artist.

abrupt gestures and too-bright eyes. His spirit of sacrifice seemed astonishing, his excessive asceticism alarming. Men pursued him with sarcasm, children feared him, and as for women — who could love this terrible man? His superiors got rid of him in July 1879.

Then began one of the darkest periods of his life, months of poverty, moral distress, anguish, roving on the roads. To his brother Theo, who was about to enter Goupil's in Paris, he wrote a poignant letter, in which he announced his decision to devote himself to painting.

In October 1880, he was in Brussels, where he studied drawing and made copies from Millet. From April to December 1881, he stayed at Etten with his parents. He experienced another sentimental disappointment there. Turned down by his cousin, Kee, he went away and settled in The Hague. The painter Mauve, another cousin of his, took him in cordially and gave him useful advice.

In January 1882, he met in the street a prostitute named Christine, who was ugly, drunk and pregnant. He took her with him. To this woman he gave all the love of which he was capable. The episode lasted twenty months, until he realized definitely that he was no better at individual love than at the love of humanity and the love of God.

From then on his humiliated pride took refuge in art. With his artistic apostolate his misfortunes grew. He quarrelled with his father, who disapproved of his artistic career. He fell out with Mauve and Israels, the teachers of The Hague School, whose teaching had finally become unbearable to him. Then, in December 1883, he returned to his father's house, this time at Nuenen, and courageously gave himself up to painting. He did studies of the heath, cottages, weavers, peasants, executed in the rough, black dismal manner of *The Loom* (1884) and *The Potato-Eaters* (V.W. Van Gogh Collection, Laren), his first large picture. His native tendency, the influence of his environment, the contagion of example—all incited him to per-

severe in this gloomy realism. How, then, can the radiant masterpieces that were to follow be explained?

In November 1885, he was in Antwerp. His father had just died. His brother Theo, with whom he had been in correspondence for five years, had sent him some money. He had discovered Rubens and the joy of life, and also Japanese fabrics, whose colors delighted him. He bought some, decorated his room with them, spent hours contemplating and studying them. He glimpsed an outlet for his still obscure desires, a new world of light, consolation, balance.

He decided all of a sudden in February 1887 to leave for Paris. Theo received and sheltered him affectionately. He was dazzled by Impressionist pictures. He met Pissarro,

Autumn Landscape.

Road with Cypress. ➡

Girl in Forest.

Degas, Gauguin, and Signac. In June 1886, he enrolled at the École Nationale des Beaux-Arts in the Cormon studio, where he made friends with Toulouse-Lautrec and Émile Bernard, who was eighteen then and with whom he kept up a regular correspondence. He worked desperately. He painted streets of Paris, portraits, flowers. He exhibited a few canvases at Père Tanguy's among others by Monet, Guillaumin and Signac. His brother, who was then the manager of the Goupil Gallery, encouraged and backed him. Obsessed by Japanese prints, he copied *The Bridge Under Rain* and *The Tree of Hiroshige.* His palette lightened; he even borrowed the Impressionist pointillist technique, as in the *Portrait of Père Tanguy* (1887, Musée Rodin) or in *View from the Artist's Room, rue Lepic* (1887).

In the pictures of Pissaro, Monet, Guillaumin, he rediscovered the light handling and the fresh tones of the Japanese. But French Impressionism had caused a decisive shock to his thinking mind. He felt such a need to emulate

the Impressionists that he did some two hundred pictures during the twenty months of his stay in Paris. This prolific and sometimes uncontrolled production includes outdoor scenes, such as *Féte at Montmartre* (1886), *Restaurant la Siréne* (1887), *Little Gardens on Montmartre* (1887), still-lifes such as *The Yellow Books* (*Parisian Novels*) and a series of twenty-three self-portraits, including the one at his easel (1888), which in a way marks the end of this period.

The winter of 1887 was an unhappy one for him. The grey sky, the gloomy streets, the sadness of the capital became unbearable to him. The Parisian painters could not give him more than he had taken from them. The rejuvenation he had received from their contact was already exhausted. He needed light, heat, to warm his frozen soul and awaken his eagerness for work. Upon the advice of Toulouse-Lautrec, he went to Arles, on February 20, 1888. In Provence everything delighted him, the orchards in bloom, the beautiful women of Arles, the Zouaves of the

Public Bath at the Seine.

garrison, the drinkers of absinthe. He exclaimed with rapture, "This is the Orient!" He was thirty-five and felt happy. With ease and enthusiasm he drew with a reed, painted well-balanced canvases, firmly arranged, almost serene. At last he had found clear-cut contours, light without shadow, pure color, dazzling, crackling vermilion red, Prussian blue, emerald green, sacred yellow, the emblem of the sun. He shed the finery of Impressionism, gave up the divided stroke, fragmented design, subtle modulations. Vigorous, precise, incisive, his line captured the inner structure of objects. He painted nearly two hundred pictures in fifteen months, executing three, four and sometimes up to five versions of some of them: *The Drawbridge at Arles, The Plain of la Crau, Sunflowers, Café at Night, L'Arlesienne (Mme Ginoux), The Postman Roulin*, his wife and their son, *Armand Roulin*. From a short stay at Saintes-Maries-de-la-Mer he brought back drawings and canvases, notably his *Barges on the Beach* (Lauren) and a *Seascape* (Moscow). He left an admirable representa-

tion of his *Bedroom in Arles* (October 1888), of which he later made, at Saint-Rémy, one replica from memory.

However, his material existence was most precarious. He did not have enough to eat. He sold nothing. He suffered from hallucinations and crises, from which he emerged dazed. The idea of death haunted him. As if he had presentiment of his approaching end, he hurried, worked furiously, in a state of exaltation that saved him from despair. His mind was on fire. His pictures dripped with golden light. He was "in the center of the universal fusion" that transmuted his colors and consumed his brain. Crises grew more numerous. He played with a project for an artists' colony that he would have called "The Studio of the South," where groups of men would work at projects in common.

Late in October 1888, Gauguin responded to his appeal. Vincent was quite cheered up. But in stormy discussions the relationship between these two opposed natures soon deteriorated. On Christmas night, during a futile

73

Riverside in Spring.

quarrel, Van Gogh threw his glass in Gauguin's face. The next day, Gauguin, walking in the street, heard hurried steps behind him. He turned and saw Van Gogh with a razor in his hand. Under Gauguin's steady gaze Van Gogh stopped, then fled to his room, cut off an ear with a stroke of the razor, wrapped it in a handkerchief and went to offer it as a present to a girl in a brothel. After two weeks in a hospital he came back to paint the extraordinary *Man with an Ear Cut Off* (January 1889).

Meanwhile his hallucinations returned. Neighbors raised a petition for his internment. His unattractive appearance, his touchy character, his whims had alienated people. He had never analyzed his illness more clearly, endured men's hostility with so much resignation, or spoken of his art with more common sense and lucidity,

but now he was considered mad. He was sent back to the hospital. In Paris, Theo, who was going to be married, became alarmed and sent the painter Signac to see him. Signac spent the day of March 24 with Vincent, who kept on painting, reading, writing, in spite of his crises. When he felt too ill, he asked to be interned at the asylum of Saint-Rémy-de-Provence, on May 3, 1889.

The Arles period was over, the most fruitful if not the most original of his career. During the year he remained at the asylum he produced another hundred and fifty pictures, and hundreds of drawings, working as one possessed, interrupted in his labor by three long crises, followed by painful prostrations. He painted *Yellow Wheat, Starry Night, Asylum Grounds in Autumn*, a few portraits including that of the *Chief Superintendent of the*

Asylum, delirious landscapes, surging mountains, whirling suns, cypresses and olive trees twisted by heat. His color no longer had the sonority of the preceding period; the yellows had become coppered; the blues darkened, the vermilions browned. In compensation, rhythm became more intense: whirling arabesques, dismantled forms, perspective fleeing toward the horizon in a desperate riot of lines and colors. What he represented then on his canvases he seems to have seen through a vertigo of the imagination. The fire lit by his hand was communicated to his brain. A feeling of failure overwhelmed him. Could his works be inferior to those of the masters whom he admired? This thought frightened him.

In February 1890, he learned of the birth of Theo's son, called Vincent after himself. "The generous Theo, so indulgent a brother, at whose expense he, the failure as an ar-

tist, the painter incapable of selling a single canvas, had been living so long! Yet, in the *Mercure de France* the critic Aurier had just published the first article devoted to his work. This tribute brought him little comfort. He felt ill, exhausted. Vigilant as ever, Theo asked Doctor Gachet to take Vincent under his care at Auvers-sur-Oise.

It was thus that Van Gogh came to Paris, on May 16, 1890, and settled soon at Auvers. Doctor Gachet attended him, showed him an affectionate friendship, served as a model for him. For Vincent had resumed painting. He did his last self-portrait, now in the Louvre, *The Town Hall of Auvers*, the *Portrait of Mlle Raroux*, that of *Doctor Gachet* (Louvre), and other works, for which he had at his disposal only a technique which had already begun to disintegrate. He feared a new attack of his illness. An unspeakable sadness invaded him. Go on working when

Landscape with Cypresses.

Starry Night.

Starry Night.

the hand refuses to obey, when the enemy within will now always be the stronger? What was the use of trying? That last Sunday in July, Vincent slipped out of the Pension Ravoux, where he was staying. He made for the fields of ripe corn, where a few days before he had painted the famous *Wheat Field with Crows.* The village was deserted. He stopped in front of a farm. Nobody there. He entered the courtyard, hid himself behind a dunghill and shot himself in the chest with a pistol. He had the strength to return to the inn, go up to his room and get into bed like a wounded animal. He died two days later, in the presence of Theo, who had hastened to his bedside. He was thirty-seven years and four months old.

Unbalanced, painful, tragic, such was certainly his life. That he suffered from neurosis and epilepsy is equally true. Like Rousseau, like Baudelaire, Van Gogh felt very vividly that his life was a failure and suffered deeply from it. He was perpetually anguished, and against his anguish he tried various means of defense: religion, humanitarianism, art. He gave himself to painting with all the more passion as he saw himself threatened by an implacable disease. Lifted out of himself by art, he was able to overcome his physical failings, or at least not to think of them too much. This unstable, high-strung, obsessed man, in unceasing conflict with society and himself, created a body of work outstanding in its concerted perfection of ends and means.

However impetuously inspired and executed it may be, this art is certainly not that of a madman. Although he put all of himself into his painting, Vincent never abandoned his very obvious concern for balance, order and reason. His shortcomings are more than offset by an activity which drew from his very failures enough vigor to fight against his weakness and live in his work. He might have sunk into mental chaos; instead, he triumphed through discipline, work and meditation. In the midst of his greatest discouragements, he retained his love of simplicity and harmony, sought a reconciliation of form and color, an abstract, coherent transposition of the world.

He gave himself an infallible system of principles and rules to reach the artistic ideal that he had glimpsed in his moments of acute insight. Each of his works was the fruit of a thought, a decision, a wish for serenity rather than for strangeness. What did he want? "Something peaceful and pleasant, realistic and yet painted with emotion; something brief, synthetic, simplified and concentrated, full of calm and of pure harmony, comforting like music." He tamed his exaltations and his impulses by the laws he had established for himself. Far, then, from being the painting of a madman, Van Gogh's is that of a thoroughly conscious artist and at the same time of a robust man, a dedicated creator. If anything, he saw too clearly. He sought always elements of a beauty of which he could find only an insufficient amount. "There is an art in the future, and it will be so beautiful, so young! . . ." What bitterness

Three Pairs of Shoes.

Still Life with the Bible and Candle.

in this cry of hope! He hoped for, prepared, made possible a golden age of painting, knowing nevertheless that he would not see it.

More assured of his victories than of profits, it was reserved to him, the discoverer and the pioneer, only to bequeath the means of success to those who came after him. In a way he triumphed over his illness, for his suicide prevented his madness. But he did not create the new art of which he had a presentiment and which he announced with moving certainty in his letters, because the moment for it had perhaps not yet come.

The sureness of his hand equalled that of his will. There is no groping, no working over, nor the slightest alteration in his landscapes or his portraits, which were almost always undertaken directly on canvas, in the manner of the Japanese. "It is not only by yielding to one's impulses," he wrote, "that one achieves greatness, but also by patiently filing away the steel wall that separates what one feels from what one is capable of doing." So Van Gogh expressed the inner duel that eventually exhausted his strength.

But if the man died prematurely, the work remains, and contemporary painting was, in a great measure, born of it. Van Gogh appeared when the Naturalist fiction was casting its last glow with Impressionism, at a time when academic conventions were collapsing, when tradition was dying of old age. With Cézanne and Gauguin, he questioned the technique of painting and in doing so prepared for the art of the twentieth century. He used the picture not to imitate appearances or humor the tastes of a cultivated society, but to recreate the world according to his own intelligence and sensibility.

While Cézanne was concerned with a new conception of space and Gauguin with composition, Van Gogh emancipated color, carrying it to its maximum intensity and expressiveness. In his canvases color reinforces drawing, accentuates form, creates rhythm, defines proportions and depth. It even acquires the value of a sign, addressing itself to the soul as well as to the eye: "color not locally true," he said, "from the realistic point of view of *trompe-l'oeil,* but suggestive of some emotion." He used it raw, dry, aggressive, in abrupt harmonies, now strident, now muted, without shades, without semitones, with cruel frankness. "I have tried to express with red and green the terrible human passions," he also wrote. But he always refrained from sacrificing color to form. And it is right that today his drawings should be admired as much as his pictures. He has left a number of them, and all of them are surprising in their simplicity and acuteness of expression, their assurance and swiftness of line, the variety of the graphic means which the artist used to transcribe on paper

◄ The Flowering Orchard.

Exit from the Church of Nuenen.

the quivering elements of his vision. And this vision was thoroughly his own, of undeniable depth and originality. He has had no direct descendants, although his influence has been felt by all modern painting: Fauves like Vlaminck, Derain, Dufy, Friesz; the Expressionists, in particular Soutine.

But Van Gogh was also a poet, a mystic, a thinker. No artist today raises more passionate an interest than he: his painting, his drawings, his correspondence. For Van Gogh lived in advance the drama of our time, a time that "now liberates and now enslaves." Nowhere is the study of the artist's correspondence more vital than in the case of Van Gogh. His letters to Theo, in addition to the intrinsic interest they have as deeply moving human documents, are indispensable to a thorough understanding of his concepts and intentions. (*The Complete Letters*, Thames & Hudson, 1958.)

Restaurant Interior.

Drawbridge Near Arles.

80

Self-Portrait with Severed Ear.

The Day of the God (Mahana No Atua).

Paul Gauguin

French painter, Paris, 1848 — Fatu-Iwa, one of the Marquesas Islands, 1903.

In the Antilles he found the answer to his quest: paradise setting with clearcut lines and hard, strong color contrasts.

Where do we come from? Who are we? Where are we going?

The Blue Idol.

Breton Landscape.

A knowledge of the circumstances of his birth, marriage and belated career as a painter is indispensable to a proper understanding of Gauguin and his work. Paul Gauguin was born in the Rue Notre-Dame-de-Lorette in Paris, the son of Clovis Gauguin, a republican journalist from Orléans, and Aline Chazal, daughter of the painter and lithographer André Chazal, and Flora Tristan Moscoso, an eccentric writer and militant socialist.

Through his maternal grandmother Flora Tristan, Paul was related to the Borgias of Aragon, who had given several viceroys to Peru. It was therefore quite natural for Clovis Gauguin to think of Peru as a refuge when Louis Napoleon's *coup d'état* forced him to leave France in 1851. He died on the journey. The family continued on its way and went to live in Lima.

Aline Gauguin was a loving mother, simple and sweet. (In 1892 Gauguin painted a portrait of her from a photograph and his recollections of her.) After four years in Peru she decided to return to France with her children. Paul was then seven years old. Aline was made welcome in Orléans by Isidore Gauguin, her brother-in-law. Little Paul was sent to a religious school in the town.

At the age of seventeen he joined the Navy, just as Baudelaire and Manet had done before him, and visited Rio de Janeiro, Bahia, Sweden and Denmark. After the death of his mother, he gave up the sea and went to work for a Paris Exchange broker. He remained there for twelve years. An intelligent, punctual and methodical clerk, he soon attained an enviable position in the firm. He made money, spent it wisely, and lived in comfort. Eventually he married a young, beautiful Danish girl, Mette Sophie Gad (1873).

Evidently Mette, a healthy, practical, steady and not unintelligent woman, thought she was marrying a distinguished man with a brilliant future, capable of bringing her happiness and security. What she wanted, above all,

The Swineherd.

Self-Portrait with Halo. ➡

was the peace and pleasure she derived from running her home and supervising the upbringing of her five children.

It was not to work out that way. Gauguin struck up a friendship with Schuffennecker, also in the brokerage business, who painted in his leisure time. It was he who introduced Gauguin to painting (1874). His period of apprenticeship was brief and he contributed to the Impressionist exhibitions of 1880, 1881 and 1882. Answering the irresistible call of his vocation, Gauguin gave up his work in 1883 in order to devote himself entirely to painting. Mette was thunderstruck and frightened.

Sick of her husband's "foolishness," feeling insecure and fearful for the future, Mette decided to take the children and go to live with her parents in Copenhagen. Gauguin went with them. He felt as much a stranger among the Danes as he was to feel at home, later on, among the Polynesians. He took his favorite son, Clovis, and went back to Paris, promising to send for the others as soon as

he could (1885). Then began one of the most unhappy periods of his life. Without money, without any hope of making any, he could not even provide for his son. But his passion for painting sustained and stimulated him. He was convinced of his power, his mission, and his genius.

In 1886 he went to live in Pont-Aven, a charming village in Brittany, but stayed for only a few months. Brittany did not give him the stimulus he had hoped for. Old visions, long dormant, reawakened in him. A year later he embarked for Panama with his friend Charles Laval. A typhus epidemic drove them away. They left for Martinique, where the revelation that Gauguin had so long awaited came to him: lush vegetation, ever-clear skies, lavish Nature, and a simple, happy existence. For lack of funds he had to drag himself away from this tropical paradise and return to France (December 1887).

Gauguin was then a man of forty, vigorous, domineering, with a noble and haughty bearing. His features are

well known, thanks to his numerous self-portraits: the narrow, prominent forehead, the blue, deep-set eyes, the hooked nose and determined chin, the thick neck that suggests heaviness and arrogant power. However difficult his character, however uncompromising his opinions, he could be extremely charming and friendly when he was not contradicted or when those he talked with inspired his confidence.

His was a strong personality, irritating and engaging, in which the rustic was mixed with the aristocratic, at heart generous and good, despite the legend to the contrary, built up and maintained by the spiteful letters his wife wrote to friends she had left in France. For this husband whom she angrily accused, of "monstrous egotism," this "unnatural father," never ceased to love his wife and to suffer because he was separated from his children. To get some idea of his real feelings, his humility, tenderness and shyness, one must read his letters. But he was an artist, a man apart, resolved to pursue his destined course regardless of what it might cost him. His social duty counted for nothing in the face of his artistic duty. And, as a result he made himself suffer as cruelly as those he loved.

Why these various stays in Brittany, Panama and Martinique? As his friend Daniel de Monfreid put it: "He went to find, in what he believed to be a country of ancient customs, an environment, an atmosphere different from our overcivilized one." In the Antilles he found the answer to his quest: a paradise setting with clearcut lines and hard, strong color contrasts.

Gauguin broke with Impressionism, which had hitherto influenced his painting (1887). On his return to France he expressed his disapproval of Monet's and Pissarro's naturalist fiction. He formulated and preached "Synthesism." It may well be that the aesthetic principles designated under this name were inspired by Émile Bernard, as Bernard claimed. But that does not matter, for it was Gauguin who first enunciated this new theory and practiced it with supreme mastery. Massive, simplified forms, flat colors, cloisonnism, shadowless drawing, abstraction of design and color, free treatment of Nature — such were the principal articles of the credo that Gauguin formulated in 1888 during his second stay at Pont-Aven, and completed in the same year at Arles (where Van Gogh revealed Japanese art to him), and at Pont-Aven and Le Pouldu (From April 1889 to November 1890). It was at this time that he painted the *Vision after the Sermon* (1888) and *The Yellow Christ* (1889). He also tried mural painting, sculpture, engraving and ceramics.

His ancestry, his childhood memories, the impressions he brought back from Martinique, his three stays in Brittany — all these gave him the incentive to renew an art that had been corrupted by the Impressionists. Eight painters grouped themselves around him, and constituted

La Belle Angèle.

Faa Iheihe (detail).

Woman with Fruit.

Portrait of Marie Derrien.

the School of Pont-Aven. Led by Sérusier, the Nabis came and joined them. Fêted in Paris by the independent critics, by writers such as Stéphane Mallarmé, the poet, and Octave Mirbeau, the novelist, Gauguin might well have been content with such a strong position. But in the midst of his court he began to feel more and more alone. Brittany had nothing more to offer him, and France was too small for him and his dream. On the 23rd of February, 1891, he put thirty of his paintings up at auction, and with the proceeds embarked for Tahiti on the 4th of April.

At Papeete he found Europe again, with its vices, its stupidity and frivolity. He went to live in Matajéa, in a straw hut, among the peaceful, ingenuous population. He joined in all their rites and games, determined to destroy whatever trace of "civilization" still remained in him. When his money ran out, and his debtors in Paris ignored his requests for payment, he was left without food, without clothes, and completely debilitated by a year of fierce, feverish work. He decided to return to France. *Women on the Beach, Vahini with Gardenia, Otahi, I raro te oviri* (Minneapolis), *When will you marry? Arearea* (Louvre), are a few of the many canvases he painted during this period.

When he returned to France, in April 1893, sick, and at the end of his resources, he found a small legacy await-

Bonjour Monsieur Gauguin.

Rural Landscape. ➡

The Bay of Saint-Pierre in Martinique.

ing him, left by his uncle, Isidore Gauguin. He had several months of happiness. Dividing his time between Pont-Aven, Le Pouldu and Paris, he soon disposed of all his money. In his studio in the Rue Vercingétorix he gave a number of noisy parties, presided over by Annah, the Javanese girl, a monkey and a parrot. The free- spending, easy-going days soon came to an end.

An exhibition of his Tahitian works at the Durand-Ruel Gallery on the 4th of November, 1893, held at the suggestion of Degas, was a fiasco from the financial point of view. But his new painting, mysterious and barbaric, aroused the enthusiasm of Bonnard, Vuillard and all the Nabis. After a series of misfortunes (including a last, painful interview with his wife in Copenhagen, and the flight of Annah, who ransacked his studio), Gauguin decided to return to the South Seas. A second auction to finance him was a complete failure. He set out nevertheless, for Tahiti, and arrived there in July, 1895.

He settled in the north of the island, and set to work immediately. And that is how the legend began, so common today, so unusual then: the legend of the European casting off civilization, alone and naked before the splendor of Nature. In October Gauguin began to have severe physical

suffering. Whenever it abated, he applied himself to his work with renewed ardor and frenzy. The year 1897 was one of great sorrow for him: his beloved daughter, Aline, died; his correspondence with Mette came to an end; he was in the hospital for a time. But it was also the year of his masterpieces *Whence Come We? What Are We? Whither Do We Go?* (Museum of Fine Arts, Boston), *Nevermore* (Courtauld Institute, London). His manuscript *Noa Noa* appeared in the *Revue Blanche*.

The following year, after an attempt to commit suicide, he went to work as clerk and draftsman in the Department of Public Works. Sick at heart, suffering from the effects of syphilis, he nevertheless had the courage to paint, draw, sculpt, engrave and write. He got himself into trouble defending natives from rough handling by the whites. He was even sentenced to three months imprisonment and a fine of a thousand francs. Finally, worn out by privations, almost unable to move, he died on the 6th of May, 1903, after executing some of his finest canvases: *Barbaric Tales, Horsemen on the Beach* and *The Gold of Their Bodies* (Louvre). The last thing he painted was a Brittany snow scene.

What Gauguin went to find in the South Seas was original purity, innocence, a way of forgetting oneself, natural man saved from the artificialities of civilization, and the universality and permanence of art. In his desire to reach the source of inspiration he reached the very sources of communication. He attained the solemn grandeur of ancient and primitive art through the immobility of his figures, the impassivity of their features, the serene gravity of their attitudes. That is why he is as close to Cretan and Egyptian art as he is to that of his contemporaries.

A creator who wanted to dominate his aesthetic adventure by the intellect, he succeeded in finding the appropriate means for realizing his conceptions. It was in order to give his compositions a monumental and, consequently, decorative character that he deliberately rejected modelling, form values, linear perspective, recession of planes, and secondary details, and neglected movement, relief, and the sensuality of expression. His South Sea canvases inspire a feeling of awe toward life, bitter regret for lost love and liberty, and a fear of the unknown, through the quiet cadence of their lines, their broad, flat areas of color, and their grave, transfixed sumptuousness.

Gauguin excelled in the art of composition. More than that, he invented a composition as different from that of the classical masters as theirs was from the composition characteristic of the Middle Ages. "Barbarism," he said, "is for me a rejuvenation." In his search he renewed pictorial art, and gave modern painting a meaning. His companions at Pont-Aven and the Nabis submitted to his leadership, and the *Fauves* were his direct heirs. Gauguin was also the one who inspired the present interest in ancient civilizations. His sculptures prepared the ground for the acceptance of Negro and Melanesian fetishes. It was he who made possible many of the gains and discoveries of contemporary art. Of all the great innovators of the nineteenth century, it is Gauguin whom many non-representational artists of today regard as their precursor.

Vision After the Sermon: Jacob Wrestling with the Angel.

IA ORANA MARIA

← *The Yellow Christ.*

La Orana Maria.

Caprice in Purple and Gold, No. 2: The Golden Screen.

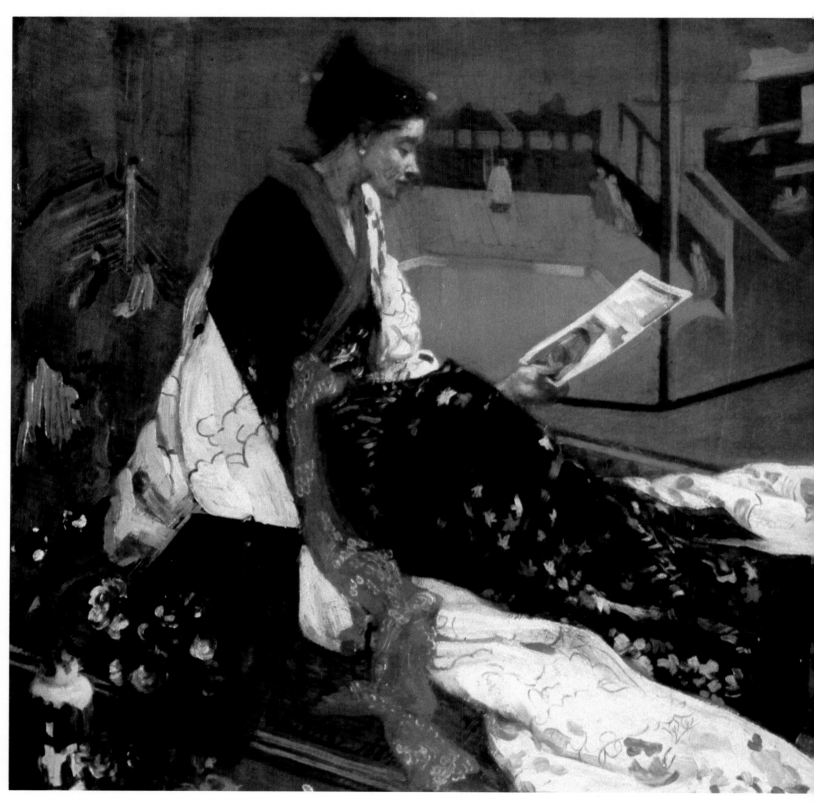

James A. MacNeill /Whistler

Lowell (Massachusetts), 1834 — London, July 17, 1903.

He had a gift for creating evocations or reveries, such as his "Old Battersea Bridge," which rises fluidly, fantastically, and "morosely," in blue and gold, above the waters of the Thames.

← *Nocturne in Black and Gold: The Falling Rocket.*

Valparaiso: Sunset in Pink and Green.

This American of Irish origin, who chose to reside in Paris and in London, was characterized by an extremely individualized form of dandyism. He enjoyed disputes and liked to be a subject of conversation — but only in low voices and within a small group. Whistler avoided the preciosity of the pre-Raphaelites. He reintroduced mirages and interrupted illusions in painting. Nevertheless, he mistrusted excessive boldness, and setting himself apart from his friends (the Impressionists), he chose to be a virtuoso of the palette.

He was Mallarmé's "strange gentleman, the prince of something or other." He would appear in the sophisticated salons of London and Paris wearing a high-collared jacket, although he never wore a cravat. He appeared to be a calm and elegantly glorious prince. He arrived late at the most exclusive dinners, and all of a sudden his vibrant and deep voice would attest his presence. "It's Whistler," his companions calmly observed.

Small and dark-haired with a white forelock, Whistler appeared as an unusual and mysterious dandy and pole-

micist, wearing a monocle with a silk ribbon and seeming to be somewhat "out of date" among the Impressionists. It was merely necessary to utter his name, "Whistler," and one could envision the moving wings of a butterfly — the monogram which he used for signing his works. He was raucous; he was a conversationalist; he enjoyed paradoxes; he became entangled in a lawsuit with Ruskin; he quarreled with Carlyle and Oscar Wilde. In a few words, he was like one of Barbey d'Aurevilly's characters.

To what extent was Whistler an Impressionist? He had a gift for sometimes creating evocations or reveries, such as his "Old Battersea Bridge," which rises fluidly, fantastically, and "morosely," in blue and gold, above the waters of the Thames.

His life? He was the son of a civil engineer, and after having studied at West Point, he painted at Gleyre's *atelier*, along with Monet, Bazille, Renoir, and Sisley. He became a friend of Fantin-Latour, who portrayed him wearing a monocle and a redingote, as a participant in the "Homage to Delacroix."

99

The Blue Wave: Biarritz.

Nocturne in Blue and Gold: Old Battersea Bridge. ➤

The Little White Girl: Symphony in White No. 2.

← *The Thames in Ice.*

Women in White

There were symphonies in white, represented by women in long dresses. There were repeated trips between London and Paris, and there was Baudelaire's admiration for his watercolors. Whistler's "Woman in White" (National Gallery, Washington, D.C.), which is one of his early works, is a concerto of white hues. This painting, which was completed in 1862, was exhibited at the *Salon des Refuses* during the following year, when it created a hue and cry, along with Manet's "Luncheon on the Grass." Whistler preceded Mary Cassatt in making a sharp break with his predecessors among American artists, because he developed an original vision of art. He said, "Like a deity with a delicate essence, as it recedes from sight." Thus, in this portrait of a young woman, he succeeded in avoiding the Mannerism of the pre-Raphaelites because of the uniqueness of his lay-out and the subtlety of his tones.

Observing the solemnity of one of these "arrangements" in white, Degas slyly remarked, "She is posing before the infinite and the eternal."

In 1865, Whistler visited Courbet, his most clearly recognizable antithesis. He was traveling with Jo, his model and his companion, and the painter from Ornans completed a portrait of this beautiful Irish woman.

Later, during the Franco-Prussian War of 1870, he met Monet and Pissarro in London. During this period, he painted scenes in London and in Venice, and there was the famous lecture, "Ten O'Clock," which Mallarmé translated and read at Berthe Morisot's *salon*.

Jacques-Emile Blanche, a portraitist who knew Whistler well, has written that, "although he claimed that he detested London, he was only contented there. He was deeply attracted to these women with ruddy skin, crowned by hair which represented a deeper shade of amber than the hair of women in Venice or Seville ... The street urchins, so comically attired in coarse fabrics, penetrating the moist fog which exalts them, and the barren, but brightly colored shop-windows provided themes for his marvelous "variations," and, along the banks of the Thames, Whistler was able to rediscover Venice, or Holland, or any other region of the world."

During his final years, Whistler returned to Paris. He and his wife (the widow of the architect Godwin) lived at 110 Rue de Bac, in a pavilion whose windows faced the convent gardens. Blanche has provided a description of its furnishings and decorations: "Just as in London, the walls were painted yellow, and there was blue and white porcelain from China — with a few chairs." Whistler's studio was located on the Rue Notre-Dame-des-Champs.

As he grew older, Whistler withdrew from life in Paris, and, when he became ill, he returned to London, where he died at the age of sixty-nine.

The Boating Party.

Mary Cassatt

Pittsburgh (Pennsylvania), 1845 — France, 1927.

*The works she created were not pas-
tiches but creations carefully thought
out according to a definite technique.*

Predisposed in favor of French culture by her family background, Mary Cassatt spent the first few years of her childhood in Paris, then went to America. A short while before the Franco-Prussian war of 1870 she came back to Paris, no doubt in the hope of learning to paint under conditions more interesting than those existing at the Pennsylvania Academy of Fine Arts. Not content with studying at the Atelier Chaplin, she went to look for inspiration in the museums in Italy (where she made a study of Correggio), in Spain, and in Antwerp (where she developed an admiration for Rubens). It was in Antwerp, a few years later, that she met Degas, who suggested that she should exhibit with the Impressionists, and also gave her guidance and advice.

 *In the Garden.*   *The Toilette.*

La Toilette.

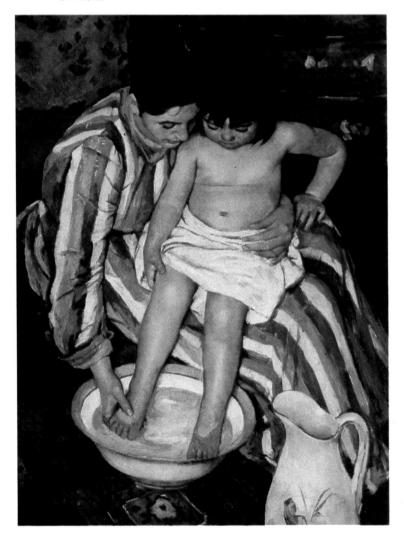

It is wrong to conclude from this that Mary Cassatt was either a pupil or an emulator of Degas. Although Degas, confirmed woman-hater that he was, relented a little towards her, and although she admired him greatly, and a certain kinship to Degas is discernible in the style and composition of her early work, Mary Cassatt mostly maintained a complete independence of technique and inspiration.

A more obvious influence is that of the Japanese artists, particularly in her drawings and drypoints. Her precise, simplified drawing has all the skill and the impressive quality of the work of the Japanese masters. Mary Cassatt had an admirable understanding of their technique and the effects that could be obtained with it. The works she

Woman in Black at the Opera.

Femme en noir.

created under this influence were not pastiches but creations carefully thought out according to a definite technique, and the majority of her works are motherhood scenes of the most tender affection. She gave this hackneyed mother-and-child theme a new freshness by stripping it of all artifice and literature. Just as the great Impressionists show us landscapes in their everyday lighting, Mary Cassatt shows us mother and child in all their simplicity, when their gestures are not made for the purpose of being seen and reproduced.

By participating in this rehabilitation of the acts of everyday life, which was a characteristic of the Impressionist movement in which she felt so much at home, Mary Cassatt made a very personal and important contribution to the body of Impressionist creation. Nearly all her energies in the last years of her life were largely absorbed in defending and making known and loved in the United States the paintings of her fellow Impressionists. She bought several paintings for herself and her family (her brother was director of the Pennsylvania railways) and persuaded her relatives to buy them too, the Stillmans, Whittemores, and particularly the Havemeyers, most of whose fine collection is now in the Metropolitan Museum of New York.

The Loge. ➡

Reading in the Garden.

Lydia Crocheting in the Garden at Marly.

Sailboats at Argenteuil.

Pierre-Auguste Renoir

French painter, Limoges, 1841 — Cagnes in the south of France, 1919.

In his work a flower, a fruit are colored, savory and palpitating with life, like a human body beneath whose skin one can tell that blood circulates.

114

Beyond Impressionism, of which he was one of the chief initiators, Renoir joins the line of artists who, from Titian and Tintoretto to Rubens, from Fragonard to Delacroix and Courbet, have seen in painting a kind of pagan and sensual celebration of the glory of woman.

The son of a tailor, Renoir began his artistic life as an apprentice, prudently painting small bouquets of flowers on porcelain plates, and then decorating, with the same care, fans and shades for missionaries. However, he had greater hopes. Having saved some money, he gave up being a workman to become a pupil and enrolled, in 1862, at the Atelier Gleyre where he met Monet, Bazille and Sisley; the nucleus of the future Impressionists was thus constituted.

The following year, leaving the Atelier, he went with his new friends to the forest of Fontainbleau to paint from Nature. He was at this time under the influence of Courbet, and this influence can be discerned as much in a work like *The Sisley Family* (1868) as in *Bather with Griffon* (1870): there is the same feeling for texture, the same sensuousness in the volumes, the same frankness. However, association with Claude Monet led him, in certain canvases, to practice the division of the colored stroke that was to be one of the achievements of Impressionism and to this we owe the two astonishing versions of *La Grenouillère*, dated 1869.

In 1870 Renoir was mobilized; he met his comrades again after the war and participated in the famous exhibition of 1874 at the photographer Nadar's where Impressionism was born. Renoir, who exhibited *La Loge*, was one of the painters who incurred the most acid criticism. This was, however, the period during which he produced works of such disconcerting beauty as *The Moulin de la Galette* (1876), *The Swing* or *Road Climbing Through the Grass* (1876). He was reproached, among other things, with covering his figures with mold when he painted sun filtering through foliage. Now that we are accustomed to colored shadow and purple tonalities, it is difficult to imagine what a great innovation a canvas like the *Moulin de la Galette* was.

The chief characteristic of Renoir's Impressionist period is that he succeeded in adding a sentimental atmosphere to the representation of Nature and seemed to be just as charmed by a tender interlacing of his figures as by the play of foliage or of water. Although he never yielded entirely to anecdote, it is evident that the subject of the canvas remained infinitely more important for him than for any other painter of the new school. While his friends were chiefly attracted by landscape, his own preference was for group studies and portraits. Having sung the joy of the popular country cafés with music and dancing, he devoted himself to producing some of the most sumptuous images of Parisian society that have been left to us by his period:

← *Spring Bouquet.* *Les Parapluies.*

for example, the portraits of the *Henriot Family* (1876), of *Madame Charpentier and Her Daughter* (1878), of *Jeanne Samary* (1877).

A painter of manners, Renoir apparently could not do without the human presence to give measure to his work and express the kind of feeling he wanted to put into it. Whereas Cézanne tended to reduce everything to the impersonal level of the object and to exercise the same calm impartiality for a face as for an apple, Renoir seemed, quite to the contrary, to bring everything into accord with his vision of man. In his work a flower, a fruit are colored, savory and palpitating with life, like a human body beneath whose skin one can tell that blood circulates. Cézanne looked and reasoned; Renoir saw and felt. The same opposition is evident in their color, in the red or warm dominants of Renoir, and the blue or green, cold dominants of Cézanne.

But Renoir's Impressionist period proper was approaching its end, and the *Lunch of the Boat Party*, which he con-

ceived during the summer of 1880, while frequenting the café of Mère Fournaise on the island of Croissy, near Paris, was one of the last canvases in which he was to express and sum up the ideal of his youth in a particularly demonstrative synthesis. He was forty and felt the need for renewal. Nothing troubled him more than the facility, the systematic spirit in which Impressionism threatened to lapse.

Renoir, like Cézanne a few years earlier, gained a fresh grip by returning to the classical tradition. He left for Italy in the autumn of 1881. After a stay in Venice, he went on to Rome, where he paused long before the frescoes of Raphael at the Villa Farnese, and then proceeded to Naples, where he discovered Pompeian painting. Of this period he would later say, "A break occurred then in my work. I had gone to the limit of Impressionism and was arriving at the conclusion that I could neither paint nor draw. In short, I was deadlocked."

Under the influence of Raphael he was henceforth to adopt a much smoother manner. Reacting against the dispersion and scattering of color in juxtaposed strokes, he gave a deliberate and rather surprising dryness to forms, which he encircled with a pure and precise line. For what had won him over in Italy, especially in Raphael's work, was the quality of the drawing, which, under a seeming coldness, lingers over the modelling of forms with a keenness and a concentration in which the roles played by the senses and the mind are difficult to separate.

Remembering that drawing represents the intellectual element in painting and color the sensory, it is not a little surprising to see a painter like Renoir adopt such a manner for a time. He who had previously required color to suggest form, to be its own design, would now imprison it in the severe frame of an increasingly minute and precise painting. This period, which has been called "Ingresque" — Renoir called it more justly his "harsh manner" — was characterized by a partiality for cold tones and acid colors, for a smooth, dull surface. A transitory stage in his work, it was nevertheless decisive in so far as it represented an admirable effort of discipline and corresponded to one of those critical moments in the life of an artist when he questions everything and thinks out his art again from its very fundamentals.

From this discipline, so contrary to his nature, Renoir was able to extract the best results in numerous canvases about 1885, notably in *Les Grandes Baigneuses* and *The Braid*. However, he did not long endure this constraint, under which his genius was visibly not developing normally, and reverted soon to his characteristic colored tex-

Girl Reading.

◄ *The Luncheon of the Boating Party.*

◄ *The Beach.* *Two Girls in a Meadow.*

Dance in the Country.

Dance in the City.

← *Lady at the Piano.*

ture. He returned to it with greater vigor than at the time of Impressionism. His experience left him with more self-confidence but, above all, with the capacity to be no longer strictly dominated by reality and to impose upon the subject treated, the will of his creative genius.

With his last "manner" one witnesses an unprecedented flowering. In a rediscovered unity of color and line, volume and light, Renoir would untiringly sing woman's body, the center of the universe, an ever-renewed creation of our desire. Nudes filled his landscapes to the point of occupying the whole canvas, and red, infinitely modulated, became the dominant color in which all the others were consumed, in the same way that woman in her eternal youth would be born again every time in Gabrielle, his faithful servant and favorite model. The compositions of this period are unusual in that under the appearance of total freedom they retain infinitely more will than those of Monet or Sisley, but more spontaneity and naturalness than those of Degas. Here Renoir has given the full measure of himself. These canvases achieved recognition very slowly, and even today many collectors consider them inferior to his earlier ones.

It is certain that the big nudes that make up the essential part of his production after 1900 represent, when compared to works like *La Loge* or the *Moulin de la Galette*, an art much more difficult to accept, for, liberated of all constraint, the new manner proved capable of transcribing Renoirs' feeling with a boldness that was not yet discernible at the time of Impressionism. The choice of themes is in itself significant. Renoir was not afraid of giving up what had made his success; when his personality was beginning to assert itself in society portraits, he rejected this theme to tackle either group studies, nudes or still-life, with which he could not be sure of conquering a new public. This attitude resulted more from his character than from an aesthetic doctrine. "For me," he liked to say, "a picture must be a pleasant thing, joyous and pretty — yes, pretty! There are too many unpleasant things in life for us to fabricate still more."

It was inevitable that the physical pleasure in form and texture that Renoir felt to an intense degree and that made him, in his own words, "pet a picture, stroke it with the hand," should draw him toward sculpture. This he undertook at a time when, unfortunately, physical disability no longer allowed him much suppleness. He secured the assistance of a young sculptor to work under his constant direction. The only sculpture entirely from his own hand is a portrait of his son Coco, which was executed about 1907-1908.

La Parisienne.

← *Odalisque.*

← *Regatta at Argenteuil.*

Her First Evening Out.

at the *Moulin de la Galette, The Swing, Lunch of the Boating Party*, or executed portraits he had been commissioned to do, it was first his own sensibility that he expressed, more than just the depiction of the sentimental atmosphere of his works, and needless to say, it was to himself above all that he meant to be true. Thus his emotions as a painter were in harmony with his feeling as a man and, as a result, an exemplary unity was established between his works, in spite of their differences.

Neither was there a sharp break when he gave up too specific subjects almost entirely and preferred to paint bathing women with naked torsos in the innumerable portraits of Gabrielle, this being his own way of creating pure painting. For here again it is clear that love of painting and admiration for women were indissolubly linked in him and were only the double aspect of his single passion for a clear and healthy life.

The case of Renoir, the sculptor, is exceptional in the history of contemporary art. It seems in fact, that sculp-

On the Terrace.   *At the Piano.* ➤

Later works were done by the sculptor Richard Guino, but Renoir's authorship of them cannot be denied; not only do they reveal a close relationship of form and spirit with his painting, but also what Richard Guino executed out of Renoir's presence cannot compare with them. The large *Venus* and the large *Kneeling Washerwoman* (1917) are masterful works that can take their place among the masterpieces of contemporary sculpture.

Renoir's is a happy art, for as a man he was without bitterness and without jealousy. His work obeyed an inner logic; it was in harmony with a perfectly balanced life able to accept itself at every moment of its development, even the most painful, when illness had deformed his limbs and in order to continue painting he was forced to have his brush tied to his wrist. The impecunious young man he had been at the beginning, who had lived in Montmartre and met the young women of the quarter, nice working girls, models, with light heads and susceptible hearts, was to be received later in families of the Parisian *haute bourgeoisie*. But, in both cases, whether he painted the ball

← *Portrait of Missia Natanson.*

Landscape.

ture, which he did not turn to until late in life when his work as a painter had already come to an end, was a way of going beyond his achievement in painting, a means of giving relief and solidity to the voluptuous forms he loved to paint. Unfortunately, when Renoir wanted to explore this new medium he was crippled with rheumatism and did not have full use of his hands.

Ambroise Vollard thought of a solution and suggested it to him; all that was required was a young artist, who would be skillful enough to interpret faithfully Renoir's ideas and modest enough to efface himself before them. The sculptor, Guino, accepted this difficult task and succeeded remarkably well. He showed such great humility that when a few years later, he wanted to do his own private work, he did not try to exploit a style he knew so well, but developed his own means of expression and nothing in his work suggests Renoir's *Bathers*.

Before collaborating with Guino, Renoir had already tried modelling on his own and had executed, in 1907, a bust and medallion of his son, Coco. These were the only works made entirely by him. The partnership with Guino began in 1913 and lasted until the end of 1918. It was in this period that Renoir's most important sculptures were done (*Venus, The Washerwoman*). He made a fresh attempt with Morel and the result was three bas-reliefs of women dancing and a pipeplayer, which are carefully modelled, but unfortunately lack the opulence of the former productions. It is obvious that the mature, serene beauty that derived from the great figures of the past had an immediate appeal for Maillol and all the artists of the movement that could be called neo-Classical.

◄ *Nude.* *Jeanne Samary.* *Girl with a Hoop.*

Nude.

Nude. ➡

The Large Bathers.

Sulking.

Edgar Degas

French painter, Paris, 1834-1917.

He cast off all that was conventional, trite or commonplace, in order to transcribe reality without having anything impede or distort his vision.

He was the son of a banker, Auguste de Gas, and, like Manet, belonged to the upper middle class by birth. His taste for classicism, the correctness with which he conducted himself, seem to be in keeping with his origins, but his exceedingly strong personality and independence of mind threw him into the camp of the revolutionaries.

He learned to paint at the Ecole Nationale des Beaux-Arts, under Louis Lamothe, a pupil of Ingres, for whom Dégas always had a profound admiration. Whatever the evolution of his genius, he was never critical of his early training.

No doubt it was his great respect for human creation that was at the bottom of the misanthropy of which he is often accused and behind which one can sense a deep tenderness. The evolution of his art explains the very special position that Dégas occupied in relation to Impressionism.

In his earliest paintings, such as *Spartan Girls and Boys Exercising* (1860), *Semiramis Building a City* (1861), and the *Misfortunes of the City of Orleans*, for which he made numerous studies, or even (a little later) the *Cotton Market in New Orleans* (1873), which he painted during his stay in the United States, we are indisputably looking at an extremely classical art, with meticulous draftsmanship. Little by little, without weakening the rigor of his drawing, he allowed color to become more and more important. Color was, however, always subordinated to a realism which would have been dry and narrow had not the genius of Dégas brought it a breadth of vision and an originality in composition which saved him from academism, and gave his work a significance far in excess of the place he is given in the Impressionist movement.

Dégas certainly belongs to Impressionism because of his desire to capture the fleeting moment, and his concern for presenting exact reality. His division of color, however, never went so far as the dispersal stressed by the landscapists. Whereas with the Impressionists, form tended to dissolve in the atmosphere, with Dégas it kept its density. In fact, unlike them, Dégas wanted to sum up the living world within strictly determined limits: he had no taste for suggesting the rustle of leaves, the shimmer of water, or the changing effects of the sky. When landscape does intrude into his composition — in his racecourse scenes in particular — it never gives the impression of a work executed on the spot, nor does one feel, with him, that Nature was necessary to his inspiration.

The picture-dealer Ambroise Vollard records this significant remark made by Dégas: "The air which one breathes in a picture is not the same air one breathes outside." He did not speak of chance beauty improvised by Nature, he preferred that created by man. He preferred the artificial light of the theatre to sunlight. He was interested in the human presence, and never treated the

Dancer in Front of Window.

← *Self-Portrait.*

133

At the Café, The Glass of Absinthe.

Dancer on the Stage. ➤

At the Theatre.

136

Woman with Chrysanthemums.

silhouettes of his figures in the casual manner of the other Impressionists. In that way his art was not a repudiation of the Classicism glorified by Ingres, but actually an extension of that formula enriched by new experiences.

All these points, on which he differed with his friends, are not, in fact, sufficient to exclude him from the Impressionist movement, in the first place, because Dégas himself decided otherwise (in fact, he participated from the beginning in a number of their exhibitions, at a time when his participation meant taking a stand, a declaration of war); but, above all, it should be understood that although he had his differences of opinion with Monet, Sisley and Pissarro, he did not oppose the new school but, with Cézanne, completed it.

Cézanne, it will be remembered, wanted to make of Impressionism a solid painting like that of the museums. One might say that Dégas dreamed of creating a museum painting as living and modern as that of the Impressionists. Whereas Monet, Sisley and Pissarro sought the maximum possibilities of color, and Cézanne did the same with respect to volume, Dégas cherished an equally tenacious passion for drawing. "I am a colorist with line," he said. He drew, and color came only to complete, by its material and fixative quality, what the drawing had caught of the dynamic reality. Drawing was, for him, the result of swift observation. It was necessary to see quickly, and the mind must be able to select; painting was the result of a series of verifications, and did not require

Woman Ironing. ➡

The Tub.

Degas

At the Milliner's.

the same inventive qualities. Slowly, however, he began to discover the wider limits of color. He began to seek in it something more than local tone, and the means of characterizing a volume.

From then on color brightened the body surfaces, caught the light on the filmy *tutus* of the dancing girls, and produced some of the most glamorous and fairylike scenes of the close of the nineteenth century. These dancers, these women at their toilet, are certainly neither intelligent nor beautiful. They are commonplace, often vulgar in their physique and in their poses, but Dégas strips them of matter, picking out only the essential rhythms of their movements, making beauty itself spring from the banality or vulgarity of their gestures. He does it so naturally, so completely, that he never gives the im-

pression of resorting to artifice in order to transfigure reality. His was a more complex, intellectual creation than those achieved by most of the other Impressionists.

One thing is certain: if Dégas, starting from Classicism, felt isolated in the midst of those who claimed to have broken with the past, he was still more opposed to those who wished to preserve it with a dismal and narrow fidelity. The deep hostility and spirit of the revolt that made Dégas reject all the academic formulas transmitted by the École des Beaux-Arts, can never be sufficiently stressed. This stubborn search for the new, the hitherto unattempted, was with Dégas more a means than an end. He wanted to cast off all that was conventional, trite or commonplace, in order to transcribe reality without having anything impede or distort his vision.

Dégas is really the first artist in whom indifference to all that was not real was carried to its extreme. His attitude is similar to that of the zoologist, or the physiologist. He outlines a human attitude as a doctor describes a clinical case. It is therefore Naturalism that transformed this traditional artist (as he was at first) into one of the most daring innovators in the transcription of the scenes of modern life.

But this search, however persistent, was never provocative. Breaking with the accepted conventions, his *Portrait of the Bellelli Family*, which he painted when he was only twenty-six, contains a real stage setting, which must have surprised his contemporaries somewhat. Dégas portrayed M. Bellelli with his back turned, seated in an armchair, an arrangement which was hardly in conformity to custom.

In his pictures of this period, no matter how traditional they might be, he seemed to be already avoiding static forms, seeking instead the effect of photographic instantaneity, which was to become characteristic of all his work. His *Cotton Market in New Orleans* (1873) is a synthesis of his art over a period of years: audacity in the placing of the subject, very important foreground, scrupulously exact draftsmanship, and a very solid, though somewhat conventional perspective. Without a doubt this very need to represent life led him to paint his characters at work, such as laundresses, milliners (1882-1884), surprising them in characteristic attitudes. For several years before then dancers had revealed to him the resources of the human body, and shown him what an artist who cared about draftsmanship could find in the acts of everyday life.

It is only natural that the name of Dégas should conjure up, for the less informed, dancers in *tutus*, practicing their points, tying their shoe ribbons, or revolving about the stage from strange perspectives with oddly foreshortened bodies. For these dancers represent Dégas' decisive contribution to the Impressionist movement. They represent the very movement of perpetually changing reality surprised, immobilized — that obsession of the artists of the period. However, the reality seen by Dégas is his own: anxious to express the maximum of life, he selected aspects of reality that had never been observed before, and were thus more striking in their truth.

His nudes — women at their toilet — reveal attitudes that do not appear very natural, the limbs being contracted in awkward gestures. For the same reason he tried to get from light effects which were contrary to natural lighting; he tried to capture the light of the footlights, which rises from the floor, inverts shadows, transforms faces, and brings gestures out in unusual relief.

Dégas went beyond this stage in the expression of movement and took up sculpture: his statuettes of horses and dancers became a real arabesque in space, and the

Two Ballet Dancers.

Portrait of Mlle. Hélène Rouart.

analogy of gesture between dancer and horse, the same way of nervously extending the leg, reveals his keen and exacting observation.

If Dégas belongs to Impressionism, it is by his technique, by his clear refusal to accept a conventional world. Study gave him a technique; the spectacle of reality gave him a sense of life.

Dégas appeared to divine the potentialities of the modern world to a far greater extent than his friends did. It is no mere accident to find in his work a forecast of new ways of disposing figures on the canvas, and unexpected angles of vision which, many years later, photography and the cinema were to use. His views seen from above, his method of depicting the main figure in a portrait off center, of giving the foreground unexpected importance in relation to the subject as a whole, of putting the emphasis on an inert and accessory detail in order to accentuate, by contrast, the expression of life in face — all these innovations correspond exactly to what the camera gives us today. In *Le Secret Professional* Jean Cocteau writes: "I have seen photographs that Dégas enlarged himself, on which he worked directly in pastel, amazed by the arrangement, the foreshortenings and the distortion of the foreground." But that is reducing too much to chance the part played by the artist, without taking into account the sharpness of his magnificent drawing, which goes far beyond instantaneous photography, no matter how exceptional that may be.

These new possibilities interested him only in so far as they enabled him to emphasize the everyday action. Dégas always refused to paint from Nature. Although, in his work, he gives an impression of spontaneity, of having captured a gesture or pose at a dress rehearsal in the theatre, or on the racecourse, his pictures are all studio productions, the results of long hours of hard work under conditions where, unlike the artist who works from Nature, he is not limited by time. His painstaking drawings were made from memory, or from "notes." At a time when some painters were proclaiming their desire to depict their passing impressions, Dégas' profound and patient observation produced masterpieces full of the feeling of life.

He brought the same research approach to the problems of technique, and there, too, his classical sense, far from limiting him, impelled him to seek that mastery of his craft which the painters of the past had had. Though he used the most varied mediums, he found pastel the one that suited him best. Sometimes he used different mediums in the same picture, or else he would superimpose coats of pastel in order to obtain, as in oil-painting, a play of transparencies between the strokes. Towards the end of his life, his sight failing, he developed a preference for working in charcoal, multiplying the sharp, nervous strokes, often enhancing them with pastel.

Mary Cassatt at the Louvre.

← *Dancers, Pink and Green.*

143

The Harbor at Lorient.

Berthe Marie Pauline Morisot

French painter, Bourges, 1841-1895.

Characteristic of her genius, are feasts of light, of aerial mobility and lightness, of a spontaneous freshness, constantly renewed.

Woman and Child Sitting in the Garden at Bougival.

Wheat Field.

The Artist's Sister, Madame Pontillon, Seated on Grass.

Berthe Morisot was brought up in cultivated but traditional middle-class surroundings. Her father was a high government official. Nothing in those surroundings would have led one to predict that from the very outset she would be drawn towards the best artists of her time.

Her temperament asserted itself at once in the reticence with which she met the mediocre teaching of her first instructor, Chocarne, in the profit she was able to draw from that of the second, Guichard; and further in the desire she expressed to work with Corot. It was under his guidance that she painted from 1862 to 1868. She assimilated his lessons perfectly, and to them she owed a great deal. Their influence is apparent until about 1874: *The Harbour of Lorient* (1869), *On the Balcony* (1872), *The Butterfly Chase, At Maurecourt* (1874). But attracted by the art of Manet, she made his acquaintance in 1868, and his influence, in addition to that of Corot, was especially apparent in the years 1875-1876: *Woman at the Mirror, Le Déjeuner sur l'Herbe.*

However, having joined the Impressionist group at the beginning, she drew Manet towards light colors and outdoor painting. It was between 1877 and 1879 that she forged her own style, which began to crystallize during this period (*Young Woman Powdering Her Face,* 1877; *Behind the Blind,* 1878; *Summer Day,* 1879). She did not resort to the systematic divided stroke but to large strokes very freely applied in all directions, which gave her canvases an aspect characteristic of herself alone. The familiar interior or open-air scenes she painted are bathed in radiant and iridescent light in which silvery tones mingle in harmonies of a rarely achieved delicacy and sensitivity.

Extremely characteristic of her genius, these paintings are feasts of light, of aerial mobility and lightness, of a spontaneous freshness, constantly renewed from 1879 to 1889 (*Eugène Manet and his Daughter at Bougival,* 1881; *The Veranda,* 1882; *The Garden,* 1883; *On the Lake,* 1884; *Reading,* 1888). This very free, personal manner seemed particularly to suit her temperament which found in it a medium made to order.

However, towards 1889 she became disturbed by the danger inherent in the Impressionist vision, which was too exclusively attached to the atmospheric aspect of the world and she sought greater unity and respect for form. She assumed a long and flexible stroke that followed the form

In the Dining Room.

without encircling it, but shaped its mass and luminosity: *The Mandolin* (1889), *Young Girl Asleep* (1892), *Young Girl with a Fan* (1893), *The Two Sisters* (1894). This is her final manner, for she died early in 1895.

Without separating it from the rest, the important place that watercolor occupied in her work should be stressed, as this medium corresponded particularly well to her nature as a painter and is one of which she made masterful use. A few simple, limpid spots, applied with extreme audacity, were all she needed to express herself com-

pletely. Specifically a painter, Berthe Morisot was responsive, above all, to the play of light upon the world which surrounded her; she drew her emotions from it, and in its pictorial interpretation she expressed her nature as a woman and an artist. She allowed no ideology or spirit of system to impair the spontaneity of her art, at whose service she put only purely plastic means. She excluded brutality, preferring delicacy, and she found her most favorable climate in the intimate atmosphere of family scenes from which she could extract poetry.

The Balcony. ➔

The Cherry Tree.

Au Cirque Fernando: The Equestrienne.

Henri de Toulouse-Lautrec

French painter, Albi, 1844 — Château de Malromé at Céleyran, 1901.

He was the first to follow the idolatrous cult of the star, an exceptional being, a superior animal who attracts all the interest in a show.

Lautrec was the descendant of a family that traced its origin back to the Counts of Toulouse, defenders of the Albigensian Cathari, and the Viscounts of Lautrec.

Count Alphonse, his father, was an original personality, passionately fond of falcon hunting, exotic weapons, horses and carriages. His disguises and games, carried out with the unalterable seriousness of a totally assured man, foreshadowed the wry humor of the painter, his absolute straightforwardness to the point of violence, his stubbornness of will, his wholehearted participation in every act of life.

◀ *Woman at her Toilet.*

Yvette Guilbert Taking a Curtain Call.

Lautrec's childhood was quite normal. Except for a short period of schooling at the Lycée Condorcet in Paris, it was spent in his family's country house. His studies were directed by his mother. He began drawing very early, filling the margins of his copybooks with caricatures of his parents, his teachers, his cousins, the animals he observed; he showed a special predilection for horses and applied himself to drawing whole sequences of the same subject, to study its variations and different aspects.

Two falls, at Albi in 1878, and at Barèges in 1879, in which he broke both legs, left him after months of immobility, completely deformed, his torso supported by two weak and shortened legs. From his convalescences came letters and travel notebooks addressed to cousins or friends, whose gaiety reveals a moving self-control. Not only did he not complain, he even stressed his disability, as if to discourage all compassion in advance. He made every effort to behave like a normal man. In his drawings, based on remarkable observation, he showed great interest in the vitality and movement of people.

Acting upon the advice of the animal painter René Princeteau, a friend of his father, he began painting and discovered a new medium in color. The influence of this first teacher lasted for two or three years, and in many respects was decisive. Being affected himself by a physical handicap—he was a deaf mute—René Princeteau presumably brought a special comprehension and attention to the formation of the young cripple.

In his first works, *Artillerymen and Cuirassiers on Horseback*, reminiscences of maneuvers that had taken place near his family's estate, Lautrec made use of an abbreviated and flexible technique of small divergent brush strokes, borrowed from his teacher, which was far from the systematic disintegration of tones of Impressionism, but which lent itself to improvisation.

In 1882, having received his family's permission to devote himself entirely to painting, he came to Paris to complete his training. He worked at first in the studio of Princeteau and underwent the influence of John Lewis Brown and Forain. In 1883 he entered the École Nationale des Beaux-Arts in the studio of Cormon, a mediocre painter who did prehistoric reconstructions, but was of a tolerant mind, and with whom he worked intermittently until 1887. It was in this studio that he met Emile Bernard, Anquetin and Van Gogh, who impressed him deeply.

In 1887, having already lived two years in Montmartre, he set up his studio in the Rue Caulaincourt, on the corner of the Rue Tourlaque. He was next door to the Goupil print shop, where he encountered Maurice Joyant, his former schoolmate at the Lycée Condorcet, who became the chief defender of his work. Lautrec frequented the ballrooms and cabarets of Montmartre, in particular the "Mirliton," where Bruant sang his social ballads and greeted his clients with offensive remarks. Lautrec il-

Jane Avril Dancing.

lustrated Bruant's most famous songs: *At Batignolles, At Belleville, At Saint-Lazare;* on the walls of the cabaret he painted dancing scenes, in which La Goulue appeared for the first time (1886); finally, under the influence of Bruant and Raffaelli, he executed realistic works: *Gueule de Bois* (1888-1889), posed by Suzanne Valadon, and *A la Mie* (1891).

Nevertheless, he did not give in to the sentimentality of the slums. He was so intensely interested in the character of his models, whoever they were, that he gave them a remarkable dignity. In the garden of Père Forest, neighboring his studio, he painted a series of portraits of women out of doors, from Montmartre models and prostitutes

whose names or nicknames are barely known: Hélène V., Augusta, Gabrielle, the policeman's daughter, Berthe the Deaf, Casque d'Or, Honorine P., the woman with the gloves.

These portraits, rich in psychological and human insight, enabled Lautrec to perfect his pictorial technique. Observing his model in the crude light of day, he accustomed himself to considering it as a whole, without any shadow whatever. He did not think, like the Impressionists, of studying the variations that the time of the day brings to things; he never resorted to chiaroscuro. For him, whose curiosity was concerned with human beings alone, light had only one role: to illuminate, not to alter vision or to make changing what is fixed and full. This is why he was led to create the cold and ideal light of which Pierre MacOrlan speaks, and which enabled him to search the face of man and to strip it of its secrets.

Thus he presented the model in a sort of moral and psychological nakedness. He did not paint the representative of a profession of a class, but a being whose destiny appears unique in his attitudes and his face. He rejected everything inessential, sometimes setting the scene precisely, but without ever allowing the setting to capture attention and play more than the environmental role assigned to it.

All the persons whose individuality he fixed can be found in the large compositions of dancing at the Moulin de la Galette and the Moùlin Rouge. Here he tried to bring out the generic features of his models and to give a collective representation of a milieu. These works obey a rhythm that transfigures them, that of the dance, and the dance itself is personified by La Goulue or Jane Avril. These faces, which haunted him or were familiar to him, took on a special intensity as they touched common life. La Goulue, with her partner Valentin le Désossé, is one of Lautrec's most powerful creations and she inspired him to do a host of drawings and pictures. For Lautrec she represented the perfect identity between the human being and his function.

The Sofa.

But outside the temple where her cult was celebrated she was no longer anything and went from degradation to degradation. On the other hand the personalities of Jane Avril, Yvette Guilbert, May Belfort, May Milton, and later of the actresses Jeanne Granier, Marcelle Lender, Berthe Bady and many others, unfolded as their art evolved. Thus Lautrec attached himself to beings whom he found exceptional and applied himself to discovering their unique features. He was the first to follow the idolatrous cult of the star, an exceptional being, a superior animal who attracts all the interest in a show. He brought out the definitive features by emphasizing them; and one can see, for example, a great actress like Yvette Guilbert become the incarnation of Lautrec's representation of her, which deeply shocked her at first.

Even more personal were the solutions Lautrec brought to other spheres of plastic expression. The appeal that theatres had for him caused him to execute, simultaneously with some theatrical settings that have not come down to us, program covers, and more particularly posters. In these productions he was no less concerned with making a work of art than he was before a canvas. Advertising, which at the beginning resorted only to a rather crude form of art, thus passed to a higher level.

Bonnard was the first to have achieved delicate harmonies of shades and subtle design, suggested to him by his taste for Persian fabrics. Chéret created illusion and obsession with lightness and verve. Lautrec's admiration for Japanese prints and the recollection of certain com-

At the Moulin Rouge: The Dance.

positions of Degas enabled him to adjust even more completely to mural requirements. He broadened and deepened his pitiless drawing and made it more effective through the arabesque of his foregrounds. His few colors were clear, and applied boldly, and at once established the composition as a whole. Thus in an extreme simplification he gave the silhouette and the movements of his subject the greatest power.

The pictures of La Goulue, Bruant, Jane Avril, and Caudieux resulted in a creation of types. The presence that commands attention on the wall with explosive force, Lautrec preserved even in his works of smaller dimensions, almost interior posters, like the pictures of May Belfort and May Milton, the Confetti poster, "based upon Jeanne

Granier's smile," and most of the other lithographs in color. In his black-and-white lithographs, on the contrary, he broke the line and produced a crumbling of form.

Lautrec's interest was not confined to the theatre, music hall, circus, ballroom and bar. With his cousin Gabriel Tapié de Céleyran, who was then a medical student, he frequented the hospital where the famous surgeon Péan operated, capturing his movements with a reporter's curiosity.

A few years later, he developed a passion for sporting circles; he followed the training of champions at the Buffalo cycle-racing track, operated by his friend the humorist Tristan Bernard, making sketches of this still unexplored world which he recreated in lithographs and posters. He

Girl in a Studio.

The Goulue Entering the Moulin Rouge.

attended the hearings of great trials. He was extremely fond of travelling and organized his tours with a personal and amusing touch, always dragging along some friend. To go to Bordeaux he embarked every year at Le Havre and took freighters going to Africa.

Once, through admiration for a lady passenger, he went on as far as Lisbon, whence he returned via Toledo, discovering in El Greco the painter who impressed him most, with Cranach and the Japanese. During one of his numerous trips to England, he fell into the midst of the tragedy of Oscar Wilde, whose prodigious swollen night owl's face he drew with a few strokes.

In the clearness of his vision, the courage of his analysis, Lautrec renewed all the themes he treated. Thus the world

of prostitution, which had already inspired Constantin Guys and Degas, furnished him with a completely new repertoire of forms. Besides, he attached the greatest importance to this subject.

But he was careful not to create a useless scandal and kept all canvases related to it secret. At his exhibition at the Manzi-Joyant Gallery in 1896, he assembled these pictures in a first-floor room to which he alone had the key, and he showed them only to visitors who asked to see them. Almost all of these works, which remained in his studio, are in the Albi Museum. In them Lautrec depicted the atmosphere of the houses with details of exact truthfulness, but as an almost normal and natural life. He was

Portrait of Désiré Dihau.

interested in prostitutes and their way of life, without ever alluding to the profession they exercised; he suggested nothing and dramatized nothing. He who hated professional models and their conventional poses found here an ideal subject of observation: the sight of nudes at liberty, unconstrained. He was interested in the types, the customs, the rules of this world situated outside common morality. He enjoyed the company of this relaxed humanity offered to his analysis. He felt at home in these houses, readily established himself there for several days, receiving friends and working assiduously, living in fraternal sympathy with these beings degraded like himself and alive like himself. This part of his work, alien to all passion or spectator's emotion, is a faithful transcription, accurate beyond all picturesqueness. These personages transcend their condition and partake of the universal.

Beginning in 1898, Lautrec's health deteriorated. Overindulgence in alcohol extinguished his prodigious vitality; his mood became irritable, the prey of horrible obsessions; he hardly worked at all. In 1899, after an especially serious crisis, he was taken to a nursing home in Neuilly for a cure. He could not bear the loss of freedom, and to prove that he was still himself, he executed from memory, by a tremendous effort of will, the series of colored-pencil *Circus* drawings, a synthesis of his most precious recollection of the rings he had frequented passionately since his youth.

Restored to normal life, he applied himself to perfecting his past work. In a final effort he undertook to renew his

La Toilette.

Woman in a Black Boa.

162

A la Mie.

La Revue Blanche.

Jane Avril.

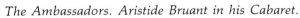

The Ambassadors. Aristide Bruant in his Cabaret.

Queen of Joy.

Confetti.

Moulin Rouge.

Ces Dames...

Jardin de Paris. Jane Avril. ➤

technique. Having started from analysis to develop a linear construction so expressive that it needed only a colored drawing, taking advantage of the natural ground of cardboard or planes of highly diluted colors, in his last works he came to paint with thick pastes and construct large planes in conflict with each other.

Toulouse-Lautrec was above all an independent. He had friends but never tried to form pupils or disciples. He hated all artistic theories and participated in no movement; nevertheless, he was completely of his time and succeeded in seizing its fundamental problems by instinct. An implacable enemy of old techniques and traditional recipes, he gave a new vision of reality, in all freedom, unconcerned with influencing anyone, and he always considered young painters like Bonnard, Vuillard or Vallotton as his equals.

While he admired Renoir and Monet, he felt infinitely closer to Degas and to Manet, who were more involved in the life of his time. For Lautrec, only the human figure counted, and he deplored Monet's early abandonment of the portrait. Later Gustave Moreau would urge his pupils to see a figure by Lautrec, "all painted in absinthe." This advice was followed, not only by the Fauves, who, after Lautrec's example, remembered that line is both drawing and color, but also by a young Spaniard, Pablo Picasso, newly arrived from Barcelona, who would draw from the work of his illustrious predecessor examples to reinforce the melancholy and disenchanted vision he had then formed of the universe. While Lautrec is, then, in his whole work, inseparable from his time, in his last works he had a presentiment of the requirements of the new century, at the dawn of which he died, on September 9th, 1901, at the age of thirty-seven.

View of the Seine.

Georges Pierre Seurat

Paris, 1859-1891.

He confined familiar forms within new profiles and raised them to an unforseeable summit of poetical expression.

Woman with a Monkey.
Study for La Grande Jatte.

A Sunday Afternoon on the Island of La Grande Jatte.

Seurat's life can best be summed up by dates corresponding to his paintings rather than to events, for the only remarkable facts of his short life are the large canvases to which he devoted all his time and immense creative powers. They represent progressive stages in a drive which led him to heights reached by only a few.

Like Van Gogh and Lautrec, who both died under forty at the end of the nineteenth century, Seurat worked feverishly and unceasingly, as though realizing that he was to be allowed only a few years in which to express himself. After attending a municipal drawing school, he endured two years' instruction at the École Nationale des Beaux-Arts before serving a twelve-month term of military training at Brest. Next he spent his time studying such masters as Ingres, Delacroix and Veronese in the Louvre, and reading the works of Charles Blanc, Chevreul, Sutter, Rood and other theoreticians of color. Blanc's assertion that "color, reduced to certain definite rules, can be taught like music" impressed him deeply, and he examined in detail Chevreul's law governing the simultaneous contrast of colors.

In 1882 and 1883 Seurat devoted nearly all his time to drawing, devising a highly individual language in black and white— the language of form rather than line, of skillfully balanced contrasts, of light and shade stripped of any incidental detail. He confined familiar forms within new profiles and raised them to an unforeseeable summit of poetical expression.

Rejecting line as a means, he composed in masses. On rough-grained Ingres drawing paper he blocked in black masses in pencil, leaving clear forms to emerge in the intervening white. By shading and perfectly balanced contrasts he revealed unthought-of resemblances. He captured light and color and transposed them into velvety blacks and expressive whites, thus creating a new world in which plastic forms emerge from dark shadow, the light parts breathe mystery, and the greys, blending black with white, disclose an intense inner life.

Flowing arabesques counter-balance one another, forms melt into or emerge from shadow, light shines forth through the mass of pencil strokes. It was an entirely new conception of drawing; later Signac described them as:

171

Bathers at Asnières.

"drawings dependent on values; mere sketches, yet revealing so fine a perception of contrast and shadow that one could paint from them direct without the model."

Just before his death he produced his only portrait—*Jeune femme se poudrant* (1889-1890) — a painting of his mistress Madeleine Knobloch (his friends knew of this liaison only after his death). Originally this canvas showed the reflection of Seurat's head in the mirror on the wall (his only self-portrait), but one of his friends, ignorant of the intimate relations between artist and model, remarked that this might lead to dubious jokes on the part of the critics, who were nearly all ill-disposed towards Seurat. So, the painter replaced his image with a pot of flowers.

Indifferent to the heated polemics which followed the exhibition of each of his works, Seurat withdrew more and more into himself, spoke little except when questioned on his theories, confided rarely even in his few intimate friends, and adopted an almost disdainful attitude towards the new recruits attracted to his circle by Signac's tireless propaganda. He showed openly that the enthusiasm of

these painters, who adopted his system and profited by his discoveries, clashed with his desire "to create something new."

However, a limited nucleus of friends gradually formed around Seurat, respecting him as their leader, and the art critic Félix Fénéon wrote articles explaining the theories of those henceforward to be known as the Neo-Impressionists. (*vide* Neo-Impressionism, also Fénéon).

In the summer of 1890, as though realizing that his days were numbered, Seurat agreed to sum up and commit to writing his theory of the concordance between tone characteristics (dark, light), colors (cold, warm) and lines (rising, descending-gay, sad). He formulated his code in the dry, precise style of a man of science rather than in the idiom of a painter:

In March 1891, a few months after having formulated these principles, Seurat was struck down by a fatal fever. "At the time of Seurat's death," said Signac later, "the critics acknowledged his talent but considered that he left no body of work behind him! It seems to me that on the contrary he gave superbly all he had to give. He would cer-

Woman Powdering Herself.

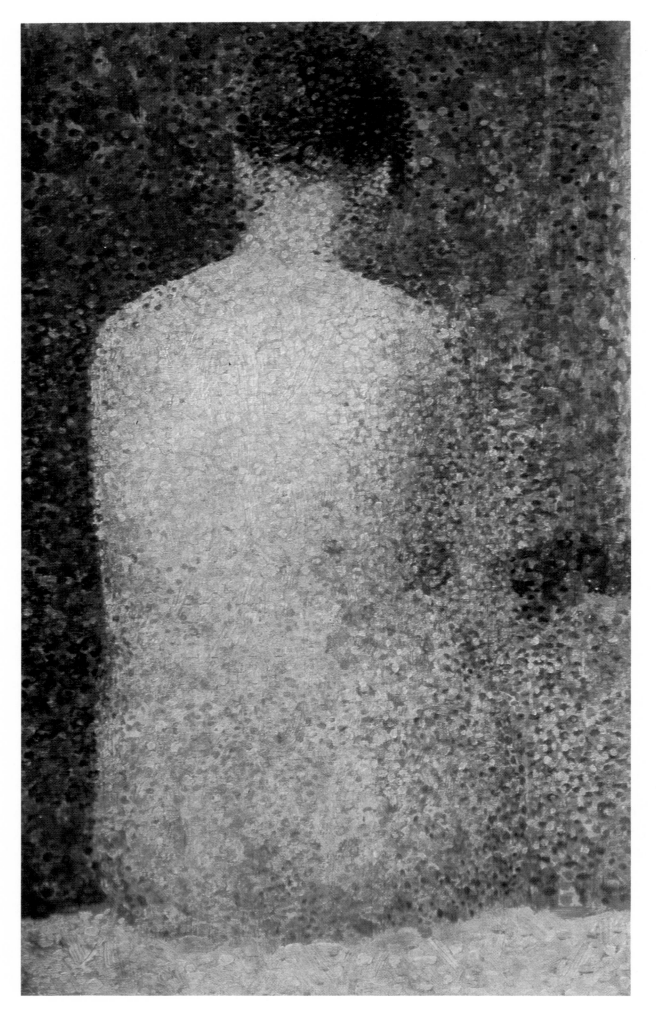

Model from the Back.

Invitation to the Sideshow (La Parade).

Les Poseuses.

Standing Model.

at the Salon in 1883; at the *Groupe des Artistes Indépendants* in 1884; at the *Société des Artistes Indépendants* in 1884-5, 1886, 1887, 1888, 1889, 1890 and 1891; at the *Blanc et Noir,* Amsterdam, in 1886. His work comprises: 170 small wooden panels, 420 drawings, 6 sketchbooks, and about 60 canvases (figures, seascapes, landscapes) among which five measuring several square meters (*la Baignade, Un Dimanche à la Grande Jatte, Poseuses, Chahut, Cirque),* and, probably, many a masterpiece."

Having thus systematically mastered the problem of black and white, Seurat devoted a year's work to his first great painting, *Une Baignade,* for which he did numerous preparatory drawing and color sketches. The picture was refused by the jury of the 1884 Salon, and their particularly uncompromising attitude that year led to the formation of the Société des Artistes Indépendants, which was to organize annual exhibitions without jury or prizes. Seurat collaborated with Signac, Dubois-Pillet and Redon in drawing up the rules of the new Society and the first Salon des Indépendants opened its doors in May 1884. Seurat exhibited his *Baignade.* Signac was immensely struck by it, but while admiring the keenly observed laws of contrast he was astonished by the dull coloring.

It was Signac who now introduced Seurat to the works of the Impressionists, explaining their efforts and pointing out the advantages of pure color, sunlight and the interplay of colors. With small, short brush strokes to interpret local color, sunlight and the interplay of colors.

Next they adopted a technique in which instead of mixing their colors on the palette they worked in tiny dots of pure color, to obtain better balance and a closer interpenetration. Seen from a distance these myriad dots revealed the color intended. From this time on Seurat's art was essentially based on the laws of simultaneous contrast (to which he later added research on the symbolic significance of line direction), the use of small dots in pure colors, and optical blending.

In accordance with these theories he proceeded to paint a series of large compositions and a number of landscapes. He explained to his friend Verhaeren that he spent the summer of each year by the sea or near Paris painting landscapes, to rest his eyesight by contact with nature, whereas in winter he worked indoors on large canvases, trying out, and if possible, resolving the problems he set himself.

In his studio he undertook successively: figures out-of-doors (*Un Dimanche à la Grande Jatte,* 1886); a reunion of people in the open air, the artificial quality of light combined with horizontal forms producing an effect of gloom (*La Parade,* 1887-1888); nude figures in the studio (*Les Poseuses,* 1888); dancing figures under artificial light, with vertical and diagonal lines accentuated to express gaiety (*Le Chahut,* 1889-1891), and the unfinished *Le Cirque* (1890-1891).

tainly have gone on and produced more, but his task was finished. He had investigated and demonstrated all his principles; black and white, harmony of line, composition, contrasts, and color harmony. What more can be asked of a painter?"

Seurat would undoubtedly have been delighted by the dry obituary notice in which his loyal friend Félix Fénéon recorded the principal dates of the artist's life: "Seurat died, on the 29th of March, at the age of thirty-one. He had ex-

The Circus.

The Gravelines Canal Looking Towards the Sea.

The Stone Breaker.

Horse and Boat.

Le Chahut.

Saint Briac.

Paul Signac

Paris, 1863-1935.

He was in his element when wrestling with problems, whether social or artistic, for they seemed to nourish his vigorous temperament eager for action.

Portrieux Roadstead.

Faubourg de Paris.

182

Entrance to the Port of Marseilles.

Signac loved life and was a man of passionate enthusiasms: for painting, science, literature, politics. Jovial and heavily built, he looked more like a Breton sailor than a painter. Vehement and impulsive in his talk, he delighted in probing problems to their depth; his every comment, in which words of kindness mingled with expressions unfit for print, revealed his intelligence, exuberance, conviction and combative nature, but even his most impetuous outbursts were never tinged by the slightest pettiness of malice.

His position was not an easy one, for he was fired with a determination to face all the issues. Yet however violent his opposition might be, it always revealed a generous mind searching for truth, ready to admit different ways of arriving at truth and accepting the validity of research diametrically opposed to his own; but both in art and in life he was the implacable enemy of flattery and pretentiousness, self-seeking and hypocrisy. Signac was in his element when wrestling with problems, whether social or artistic, for they seemed to nourish his vigorous temperament eager for action.

His middle-class family put up no resistance to his early decision to take up painting. At the start he was influenced by Monet — at that time not yet widely appreciated as an artist — and in 1884, at the age of twenty-one, he became one of the founders of the Société des Artistes Indépendants with Georges Seurat and others, and exhibited for the first time in their salon.

Seurat and Signac became intimate friends and were soon to collaborate in formulating the theories of Neo-Impressionism, the most important and revolutionary art movement of the late nineteenth century. They quickly rallied to the cause a small circle of friends of varying degrees of talent, such as Camille Pissarro and his son Lucien, Henri-Edmond Cross, Maximilien Luce, Charles Angrand, Hippolyte Petitjean, Theo van Rysselberghe, Albert Dubois-Pillet and a few others.

Road to the Customs House at Saint Tropez.

Signac was the driving force of the group, trying at all costs to attract adherents, untiringly professing his creed in discussions and by letter. After the premature death of Seurat in 1891 he undertook the difficult task of continuing the struggle for their ideals as leader of the group.

Signac had a passion for sailing, which led him to visit and paint nearly all the French ports. He sailed to Holland and Corsica, travelled to the Alps, Italy and Constantinople. For many years his base was Saint-Tropez, which he "discovered" as he also "discovered" Port-en-Bessin and Collioure. From all these ports of call he brought back innumerable watercolors, in which line and vibrant color fuse spontaneously to seize the changing aspects of nature.

Afterwards, in the studio, he used these quick sketches for the preparation and execution of large canvases, in which his aim was to balance the different elements of nature in order to achieve what he called "the most harmonious, luminous and colorful result possible."

Félix Fénéon, a friend of Signac's from the start, described his painting: "His colorings spread out in spacious waves, tone down, meet, fuse, and form a polychromatic design similar to a linear arabesque. To express these harmonies and oppositions he uses only pure colors.

Arranging these on his palette in the order of the spectrum, the painter mixes only contiguous colors, thus as far as possible obtaining the colors of the prism, adding white to graduate their tone scale. He juxtaposes these dabs of

Woman Dressing, Purple Corset.

paint on the canvas, their interplay corresponding to local color, light, and varying shadows. The eye will perceive them mixed optically. The variation of coloring is assured by this juxtaposition of elements, its freshness by their purity and a brilliant lustre by the optical blending, because unlike a mixture of pigments, optical mixing tends to brightness."

Of insatiable curiosity, Signac threw himself into the study of Chevreul's optical laws and often wrote on behalf of these theories. He wrote *From Eugène Delacroix to Neo-Impressionism* (1899), the vital textbook of the Neo-Impressionist movement, a study on *Jongkind*, a lucid essay on *The Subject in Painting (Encyclopédie Française*, vol. XVI, chap. 2), an introduction to the catalogue of an ex-

hibition *Seurat and his Friends* (Paris, 1934), as well as a Diary, of which the entries for the years 1894 to 1899 were later published in the *Gazette des Beaux-Arts* (1949-1953).

As though these multiple activities were insufficient to occupy his ebullient temperament, Signac accepted the presidency of the Société des Artistes Indépendants in 1908 and for twenty-six years worked untiringly in the service of his friends, encouraging the younger generation (he was one of the first to buy a picture by Matisse) and advocating the principles of his conception of art. His vigorous personality, which always pushed him into the limelight, may have sometimes caused his contemporaries to overlook the fact that this active, dominating man was also a talented painter of great poetic sensibility.

La Salle-à-Manger.

186

La Bouée Rouge.

Paul Cezanne

French painter, Aix-en-Provence, 1839-1906.

He was eager for honors yet indifferent to fame, small in his life yet sublime in his art, gnawed at by doubts about his work convinced of his superiority.

Cézanne came from a long line of artisans and small tradesmen of Piedmontese origin. He went to a primary school, then to a religious school, and was later sent to college by his father, who, by that time, had left his hatter's shop to become manager of a bank. Cézanne left college in 1858, with a sound education, his religious faith intact, and a close friendship with his fellow-student Émile Zola. Having done well at his studies, he entered a law school, in compliance with his father's wishes. This did not prevent him from carrying on with his drawing classes, which he had been attending since 1856. Hard-working, conscientious, but sensitive and exuberant, he was not a very gifted pupil.

He was short, thick-set, very dark, with an unprepossessing face, obstinate forehead, an aquiline nose, a keen glance and quick gestures. He enjoyed swimming, hunting, and long rambles through the countryside, was fond of music, and played the cornet in the students' orchestra, in which Zola was a flautist.

In 1859 his father acquired a seventeenth-century country house, the Jas de Bouffan, on the outskirts of Aix, and spent the summers there with his wife, his son and his two daughters. There Cézanne set up his first studio. He had already made up his mind about his future; despite his father, he was going to be a painter. His father, who intended that Paul should succeed him as head of the bank, admonished him in the following words: "Think about your future, my boy. With genius you die; it is only with money that you live"—a "bourgeois" conception of life that irritated Paul considerably, but in which he nevertheless acquiesced.

He went on painting secretly, giving his legal studies only moderate attention. Émile Zola, who had settled in Paris, urged him to come and join him there. Cézanne's father opposed the idea. But in April 1861, realizing his son's unfitness for business, and under pressure from his wife and eldest daugher, Marie, he finally gave his reluctant consent.

And so Paul Cézanne went to Paris. He took lodgings in the Rue des Feuillantines, studied at the Académie Suisse (*), became friends with Pissarro and, later, Guillaumin, and resumed his former intimacy with Zola (*). He was just about able to exist on the 125 francs which his father sent him each month. The tumult of Paris was not at all to his taste, and he was far from satisfied with the first works he produced. Eventually he was refused admission to the École Nationale des Beaux-Arts, on the ground that he had ("the temperament of a colorist") and painted "with excess." Discouraged, he went back to Aix, to the great delight of his father, who offered him a position in the bank.

But Paul, far from sacrificing the brush to finance, went on sketching and painting with ardor. He painted four large panels, *The Four Seasons*, on the walls of the Jas de

← *The Blue Vase.*   *Autoportrait.*

Gardanne and the Mt. S. Victoire.

Bouffan (today in the Petit Palais Museum in Paris), parodies that he irreverently signed "Ingres" just for the fun of it. He painted a portrait of himself and one of his father. In November 1862 he went back to Paris. He associated with the Impressionists without, however, being carried away by them. He made the acquaintance of Monet, Degas and Renoir, but the works he admired most were those of Delacroix and Courbet. Cézanne's own work at that period was very romantic. It pleased him no more than it did anyone else. In fact, nothing pleased him, and he was ill at ease everywhere, breaking off a budding friendship, avoiding a famous artist whose work he liked, changing his lodgings constantly, leaving Paris in disgust and going back to it out of curiosity, retiring to Aix and then leaving it soon after.

When his work was rejected by the Salon in 1866, he left for Aix, disgusted. He was back in Paris in the winter of 1867-68, in new lodgings, naturally. He put in brief appearances at the Café Guerbois (*), where he met Renoir, Manet, Stevens, Zola, Cladel, Duranty . . . He never felt comfortable there. His *Grog au Vin* or *Afternoon in Naples* was rejected by the Salon in 1867. That same year he met Marie-Hortense Fiquet, a young model, whom he took with him to l'Estaque when he went there to hide in 1870, to escape the draft.

After the war, he settled in Paris. He was thirty-two years old. Until then he had indulged in a violent, sombre, and theatrical kind of painting, in which his sexual obsessions and distraught dreams figured. He painted landscapes, still-lifes and portraits — of Zola, Achille Emperaire, and Valabrègue — but also death scenes and orgies, weird, fantastic scenes with a thick impasto brutally applied, where sickly blues and livid whites slash the gloomy backgrounds. Tintoretto, Magnasco, Crespi, Goya, Daumier, all the great baroque painters, seem to preside over these lyrical effusions, these convulsed forms,

The Gulf of Marseilles Seen from l'Estaque.

The Gardener (Vallier Seated). ➤

The Black Clock.

Un Dessert.

Montagnes Vues de l'Estaque.

Italian Girl Leaning on her Elbow.

Portrait of the Artist's Father.

Portrait of the Dwarf, Emperaire

these trite colors, over all the works that gave satisfaction to his turbulent nature. *The Abduction*, and *The Temptation of Saint Anthony*, *The Negro Scipio*, *The Magdalene*, or *Grief* and *The Modern Olympia* (the latter two in the Louvre)—these were the works that Manet condemned when he said to the Impressionist Guillemet: "How can you like messy painting?"

In 1872 Hortense Fiquet bore him a son to whom he gave his own name, Paul. He settled at Auvers-sur-Oise, where he lived for two years in the company of Pissarro and Guillaumin who gave him advice and influenced his work. He abandoned his wild, lusty manner, his palette became lighter, his strokes gained in precision, and he employed simpler methods. *The House of the Hanged Man* (Louvre) and *Doctor Gachet's House* (Kunstmuseum,

Basel) mark this renewal, brought about as much by a prolonged contact with Impressionism as by a personal need of order.

Cézanne made the acquaintance of Van Gogh. Doctor Gachet (*) gave him encouragement, and some astute connoisseurs bought a few of his canvases. On his return to Paris he found the Impressionists once more, at the Nouvelle Athènes (*). He exhibited with them, although not very welcome, at the first Impressionist Salon at Nadar's in 1874, which was greeted with sarcasm and jibes. Cézanne naturally came in for his share, even more than his share. On the other hand, Count Doria bought his *House of the Hanged Man*, and a Government official, Victor Chocquet (*) became his admirer, his confidant, and, on several occasions, his model.

House of the Hanged Man.

From 1874 to 1877, in a studio that he rented at 120 Rue de Vaugirard in Paris, he enjoyed a period of tranquility and productivity. The *Pool at the Jas de Bouffan* (1874) still belongs to his Impressionist style, but his *The Sea at l'Estaque,* painted during the summer of 1876, is constructed according to the principles of a new classicism, an evolution confirmed by the opulent still-lifes which followed, the various portraits of Madame Cézanne, and a series of *Bathers.* He gave up small brush strokes and the division of tones, and painted in masses. He accentuated volumes, and sought unity of composition. His work gained in thought, firmness, and plastic intensity. But he was growing bitter, and found it increasingly difficult to tolerate the company of men and worldly vanities. Truly generous and kind by nature, everything—no matter how trifling— irritated him, and he suffered very much when his ingenuous pride came up against an obstacle. That is why the annual rejection of his canvases by the Salon, the raillery of the students at the École des Beaux-Arts, and the persistent incomprehension of the public, intensified his hypochondria. He sent sixteen canvases to the 1877 Impressionist exhibition. The reception was as hostile as in 1874. His father, who had never approved of his artistic career, nor of his liaison with Hortense Fiquet, reduced the already meager allowance that he made him. That made Cézanne tend to isolate himself even more, to withdraw into himself. He exasperated his mistress with his unreasonableness, his friends with his caprices. Nevertheless, many of them remained devoted, among them the painter Guillemet,

La Montagne Sainte-Victoire.

who succeeded in having one of Cézanne's pictures exhibited at the Salon of 1882. From then on he lived in Provence, leaving it only for essential trips to Paris, or when he was invited to La Roche-Guyon by Renoir in 1885, or to Hattenville in 1886 by Victor Chocquet.

In 1883 he made the acquaintance of Monticelli. The two artists wandered through Provence on foot, haversacks on their backs, painting side by side, preferably in Gardanne, a little village in the South of France quite close to Aix-en-Provence. In 1886, in the presence of his parents, he married Hortense Fiquet, although he no longer had any feeling for her. In October of the same year his father died, at the age of almost ninety, leaving him almost two million francs, a considerable fortune in those days. Feel-

ing only repugnance for human society, Cézanne devoted himself exclusively to painting. He had broken with Zola in 1886. His wife and his sister kept house for him and supervised his son's education. In 1888 he went to live in Paris for a year. He frequently met Van Gogh, Gauguin and Émile Bernard, although he did not care for them very much. He retired finally to Aix, leaving it only for brief trips to Fontainebleau, Giverny, Vichy or Paris.

His irascibility increased with the first onset of diabetes. Without any serious reason, he quarrelled with several of his friends, particularly Claude Monet. He painted feverishly, but continued to have doubts about his work. Yet there never was so well-balanced and serene a period in his career as the ten years between 1885 and 1895. That

Houses in Provence.

was when he painted *The Chest of Drawers* (Munich), *The Blue Vase* (Louvre) and *Mardi Gras* (Moscow), the *Portrait of Gustave Geffroy*, the three versions of the *Boy in the Red Waistcoat* and the series of portraits of Madame Cézanne. He also painted five versions of the *Cardplayers*, the last of which is in the Louvre, and more than ten versions of *Bathers*, which he treated in the manner of a geometrical problem, striving to determine the laws that governed the composition of the picture.

In landscapes his favorite themes at that time were the family property, Jas de Bouffan (he painted its avenue of chestnut trees several times), the village of Gardanne, the Gulf of Marseilles, as seen from l'Estaque (one version in the Louvre) and *Mount Sainte-Victoire*, notably the one

with the big pine tree; in all, more than 250 canvases. His perseverance, if not his stubbornness, was beginning to bear fruit. This was not yet fame, but he was acquiring a reputation. One of his works was shown at the Exposition Universelle in 1889, thanks to the intervention of the faithful Chocquet. When the Théodore Duret collection was put on sale, Claude Monet bought *Village Street* for eight hundred francs, while the dealer Ambroise Vollard (*) exhibited 150 of his works in his gallery in the Rue Laffitte in 1895. The Press was outraged and the public incensed. The academicians turned up to voice indignant protest, but Cézanne's reputation emerged from this experience considerably enhanced. A number of independent painters and new connoisseurs voiced their ap-

Les Grandes Baigneuses.

Portrait of Victor Chocquet. ➤

preciation. Although he was isolated within the walls of his own mistrust, and overcome with grief at the death of his mother, his lyricism increased and his art glided towards the housekeeper, Madame Brémond.

In 1902 he had a studio built in the Chemin des Lauves. Age, and the suffering his illness gave rise to, made him even more suspicious and irritable. In 1905 he completed his *Grandes Baigneuses* (now in the Philadelphia Museum), which he had begun seven years before. On the 15th of October, 1906, overtaken by a storm while out painting, he caught a chill and collapsed. He was brought home in a cart, and Madame Brémond hastily summoned his wife and son. They arrived too late. Cézanne died on the 22nd of October.

Despite the hostility of the public and of academic circles, Cézanne's fame had continued to grow. After

Victor Chocquet's death, seven of Cézanne's canvases were sold for 17,600 francs. One of his landscapes was acquired for the Berlin Museum. He took part in the Exposition de la Libre Esthétique in Brussels in 1901, and in the Salon des Indépendants in 1899, 1901 and 1902. An entire room was reserved for him in the Salon d'Automne of 1904. He also exhibited in that Salon in 1905 and 1906.

He had triumphed at last. He was accepted by the public, admired by the younger generation, and surrounded with sympathy and veneration. Painters, writers, poets came to Aix to pay homage. Nevertheless, Cézanne continued to live simply in morose and hard-working isolation, revolutionary artist and reactionary citizen; for the boldest precursor of modern art was, at the same time, the most conservative of French bourgeois. He used to go

Man in a Cotton Cap.

to Mass every Sunday, and scrupulously observed all the conventions of the bourgeois, conservative society to which he belonged. He had an unexpected respect for people with official standing and for State institutions. One of his lifelong desires was to be admitted to the very official Salon, already looked down upon by good painters, which kept its door obstinately closed against him. He longed to be decorated, and the novelist Octave Mirbeau tried hard to get him the Legion of Honor, but in vain.

Cézanne's reserve in matters of love was proverbial. His one sentimental venture was disappointing and abortive. In fact, women frightened him. Timidity, clumsiness and shyness formed impassable barriers to his passionate temperament, as both his correspondence and his early works bear testimony. Violent and timid, churlish and kind-hearted, reserved and generous, passionate and level-headed, faint-hearted and proud, brimming over with affection yet distrustful of it in others, eager for honors yet indifferent to fame, small in his life yet sublime in his art, gnawed at by doubts about his work yet convinced of his superiority — such was Cézanne, the most balanced of painters and the most torn by contradictions; for, having repressed his instinct, he could feel it stirring tumultuously within him. There was a continuous struggle between the will to organize and the impulse to improvise, between the exigencies of a classical conscience and the pressure of a baroque temperament.

Up to 1873 his southern impetuosity and erotic imagination, a fever of subversion and the naïveté of the self-taught, produced a pictorial licentiousness, the dangers of which Cézanne soon perceived. For a while, under the influence of the Impressionists, hoping to get rid of the waywardness of his youth, he tied himself down to a discipline, and subjected his imagination to the laws of Nature.

Then began his classical period. The secret of style was no longer to be found in the delicate play of light or the banal imitation of appearances, but in the severe ordering of forms and the right distribution of colors. In his still-lifes, his portraits, his *Cardplayers*, and his views of l'Estaque or Gardanne, he resorted to an aesthetic system whose principles and appropriate means he discovered for himself; principles and means that issued from his need for perfection, his painful, groping search for an absolute.

We have now to examine Cézanne's contribution to the art of painting, a contribution so rich and weighty that it has influenced the whole of modern painting, nourished all the movements that seek renewal, and inspired all the talent and genius of our century.

To understand properly the prodigious upheaval wrought by Cézanne (since, after him, a radical change occurred in the manner of seeing and in the manner of painting), he has to be seen in relation to the painting of his time. Although he is indebted to Pissarro for freeing him from the excessive romanticism of his youth, developing his gift of observation and his color sense, nothing was more opposed to his ambition than the empiricist ideal of the Impressionists. He was a Realist as much as they were, even more so, for he wanted to go beyond the "simple sensation" and the immediate data of the senses. "To make of Impressionism something as solid and durable as the paintings in the museums," he once said.

By sheer will-power and meditation he rediscovered the innate freshness and vigor of sensation, the fundamental sensation that he wanted to make strong and permanent. He built a world whose form, construction and color ensure permanence and universality. Although he was an ardent admirer of Poussin, Daumier, and Courbet, he wanted none of that form drowned in chiaroscuro and modelling. On the contrary, he disengaged it, encircled it, put it in evidence and accentuated its internal structure. He gave consistency even to air, mist, vapor, to the most volatile and least palpable things in the universe. The sky and sea in his landscapes have as much breadth and solidity as the trees, rocks and houses. "Nature must be treated through the cylinder, the sphere, the cone," he said, as the Cubists were to repeat later.

But reality has three dimensions. How can it be represented on a flat surface? This is where the organizer comes in. With a firm and careful hand, he ordered and combined in the space of the picture the cubes of his houses, the architectures of his trees, the concrete blocks which are his people, the spheres that are his fruits. Verticals and horizontals intersect at right angles to give an effect of magnitude, balance and serenity. Realizing that Nature is "more depth than surface," he suggested the third dimension by arranging planes in an unexpected manner, by displacing the visual angles, by raising the horizon line (as in *The Sea at l'Estaque* in the Louvre), without bothering about the rules of perspective as taught in the academies.

But this tireless and exacting genius wanted to render Nature in its totality. How was he to express, at one and the same time, things and the air that envelopes them, form and atmosphere, without resorting to the chiaroscuro of the classical painters, or the soft variegations and the shimmering glints of the Impressionists? Rejecting current conventions, Cézanne made a discovery which was to have a far-reaching effect on Western art: light and shadow no longer exist. From now on they are expressed with the aid of colors. Tone takes the place of modelling of form; the relationship of colors takes the place of chiaro-

The Bathers.

Pomegranate and Pears.

scuro. He respects local tone. He substitutes pure tone, and contrasts of pure tone, for the mixture, gradations and modulations of color. "Model by the colors," said Antonello da Messina.

This suggestion, taken up by the Venetians, has become a definite acquisition, thanks to Cézanne, who invented pictorial light as different from natural light as a picture is from Nature itself. The difficulty lay in finding exact tones, and the exact interrelation of tones. This difficulty Cézanne triumphantly surmounted. In doing so, he arrived at a new interpretation of volume and drawing. Since form is created gradually by the brush as the artist works, it follows that drawing and painting cannot be distinct from each other. "When color has its richness, form has its plenitude," is his famous saying. From that time on the Impressionist division of tone began to give way to the juxtaposition of two opposite tones, the proxi-

Le Château Noir.

mity of warm and cool. Each spot of paint becomes a colored plane, a small, dense, rough-grained mass, placed there by a hand guided by reason, yet full of sensuality and flavor.

Cézanne wanted to be a painter to the exclusion of everything else. Nothing counted in his eyes except painting. "Be a painter," he wrote to Émile Bernard, "and not a writer or a philosopher." Disdaining literary subjects, genre scenes and allegorical compositions, he preferred to paint common objects, familiar landscapes, and portraits of humble folk. He did not create his *Bathers* to glorify the splendors of the flesh, or to follow a fashion, but in order to seek new forms and new plastic rhythms. Passionately a painter, he made the picture a concrete and complete world, a reality which is an end in itself.

From this it is easy to understand the profound influence he has exercised over the generation that followed him.

He brought them a method, a perfect creation, the "picture": that is to say, an architecture of tones and forms which is not an analysis of the passing moment, does not represent an anecdote or a chance incident, but is a coherent reality, indestructible and eternal. Cézanne never wanted to betray Nature. He found in himself the heritage of the old masters, which he took and enriched with his own discoveries, and exalted to the extreme limits to which his indomitable courage and genius could bring it. "To do Poussin over again from nature . . . To make of Impressionism something solid and durable like the art in the museums" — that, in short, was his credo.

His work is a lesson in energy. It gives us a profound sense of comfort, religious feeling, joy mingled with sadness. For beyond this robust and balanced art his suppressed instincts rumble, and the man groans, torn

The Mountain of Marseilleveyre and the Island of Maire.

between the classicism he has so patiently sought and his latent baroque tendencies. Hence the rickety tables, the crooked vases, the tottering chairs, the stiff limbs, the squint-eyed faces, the sloping postures, the forms that crumble when the vertical and horizontal break, the seeming awkwardness, the distortions that have for so long given Cézanne's hostile critics food for condemnation.

In the last ten years of his life the baroque invades his work without ever overstepping the limits laid down by a lifetime of conscientiousness and effort. He paints still-lifes swaying on slippery supports, views of Mount Sainte-Victoire shaken by internal fires, trees which seem struck by lightning, *Château Noir's* flaming beneath stormy skies. Fauvism is already there, just as Expressionism was in the *Temptation of St. Anthony* (1867), and Cubism in the *Cardplayers*. Who of the masters of modern art has not turned to him when in doubt and drawn comfort and

inspiration from his example? Matisse, Derain, Vlaminck, and many others have. "We all start from Cézanne," Braque, Léger and Jacques Villon declared in 1953. On the other hand, the neo-classicists claim him as their model in so far as he remained faithful to the naturalist tradition. Precursor of pure painting, but also promoter of an intellectual adventure that still continues today, Cézanne is a valid source for the non-realists as well as the realists.

There is not a painter today who is not indebted to him. Destiny chose this torn creature with the anguished heart and confident mind to weave the threads of a new tradition. "I am the primitive of the way I have discovered," he wrote one day, in the full consciousness of his originality. There have undoubtedly been other originators who have had something to give the painters of today, but they are only predecessors. He is the ancestor, the father of modern painting.

Les Nympheas.

Claude Monet

French painter, Paris, 1840 — Giverny, 1926.

The art of the painter consisted in choosing one moment in preference to another, in order to fix its individuality in a definitive image.

Haystacks at Sunset.

Haystack in Winter.

Antibes.

Claude Monet is the most Impressionist of Impressionists, and his work is the symbol of the movement. It is appropriate that one of his pictures, exhibited in 1874 and called *Impression, Sunrise* should have led a Parisian columnist to baptize the new movement. The title of the picture was in itself significant. It revealed the artist's will to transcribe his own feeling rather than to represent a particular landscape; and such an act was revolutionary in its time.

This was the point at which modern art broke with that of preceding centuries. It is likely that the persons concerned did not fully appreciate the radical change that their new attitude constituted; they did not foresee its consequences, but kept enough faith to continue their efforts in spite of the greatest difficulties. In his youth Monet had met Boudin at Le Havre and then made friends with Pissarro at the Académie Suisse where the two of them

worked. A few years later he entered the Atelier Gleyre where he met Renoir, Bazille and Sisley.

Thus, Fate brought together fortuitously the men who would soon shatter the formula in which official art was imprisoned. For several years, however, they were not so uncompromising as is thought today. Monet sent works to the Salon that were not always refused. The first painting he sent, in 1865, was accepted, and even enjoyed some success. Furthermore, he was admitted several times in later years, although of course with more difficulty.

In addition to his landscapes, Monet executed a few figure studies at this time, first a large composition, *Le Déjeuner sur l'Herbe*, which he destroyed after it had been criticized by Courbet (an admirable sketch for it survives in the Frankfurt Museum), the *Portrait of Camille*, which attracted much attention at the Salon of 1866, *Women in*

Bathers at La Grenouillère.

Bazille and Camille. ➤

the Garden, in the Louvre, and *Lunch in an Interior.* These canvases, together with a few portraits executed at various periods, are almost the only works in which he gave himself over to the representation of the human figure. This indifference may seem surprising and be regarded as a sign of insensitivity, but a more accurate interpretation suggests that for an artist as scrupulous as Monet — and scrupulousness is characteristic of the Impressionists — the portrait added psychological problems to purely pictorial ones, and that he preferred the more neutral theme of the landscape. Pictorial problems were important enough in themselves for Monet not to want to complicate them still more.

He then went through one of the darkest periods of his life. His circumstances became increasingly difficult. His goods were disdained and he saw two hundred of his paintings sold by auction in lots of 50 frs. each. He was twenty-seven years old. In despair, he tried to commit suicide, but his faithful friend, Bazille, helped him to get over his difficulties and failures. Even the work he sent to the Salon of 1869 was refused. The same year, he went with Renoir to Bougival, where together they painted the baths of La Grenouillère.

When war broke out, Monet left for Trouville, then for London, where he found Pissarro again, admired Turner's painting with him and made the acquaintance of Durand-Ruel. Returning to France in 1872, he went to live at Argenteuil where he made a studio-boat for himself from which he could study at leisure the play of light on water.

A suggestion that Bazille had once made came back to him and he invited his friends to form a group and exhibit their work together. They did so in 1874 at Nadar's, but the exhibition, now famous in the history of art, only caused derision and the most malicious comments. To the stiff and static art, manufactured in studios, that was then in favor, Monet opposed a fluidity captured from Nature: not only the fluidity of movement but also that, much more subtle, of environment and atmosphere. Had he been content to seek lifelike postures for figures, like those revealed in a candid photograph, his theories would no doubt have been accepted, but what he wanted to paint was the glow of light, the shimmering of water, the transparency of the atmosphere, the scintillation of the foliage.

His idea of the instantaneous concerned not forms in motion but an arrest of time: a landscape is not the same at dawn and at twilight, in autumn and in spring. He wanted to paint the sun, the cold, the wind, the mist. These ideas were new and came as a revelation. Oscar Wilde later remarked of him that Nature certainly imitates art, since although nobody before Claude Monet had ever discovered that fog becomes iridescent around the London bridges, nobody could afterwards see London fog without thinking of him.

Thereafter, Monet confined himself almost exclusively to landscapes, and mostly to those in which water adds an element of movement. Channel ports, the banks of the Seine, England, Holland, and Venice furnished him with inexhaustible themes until his death.

Today it is difficult to understand that this art, full of freshness and youth, sensitive to the charm of all seasons, luminous as a song of joy, could have raised storms and brought many years of poverty to its apostle. But his tenacity succeeded in convincing the unbelievers and, about 1880, Monet began to see hostility subside. Calm entered his life little by little and, later, comfort and even wealth with the fame that crowned his old age.

However, the crown was not untarnished, for if Alfred Sisley had died too young to see the beginnings of his success, Monet lived to witness the new assaults that triumphant Impressionism was to undergo, this time not from official or academic artists but from the members of the new generation who, making use of the freedom won for them by the Impressionists, rejected them to explore other paths towards other feats of daring, other concepts, even other repudiations. The Impressionist technique, carried to the point Monet finally reached, can undoubtedly be criticized for giving less importance to forms than to the atmosphere enveloping them. But an artist cannot be denied the right to think his thought through to the end. Monet was not afraid to seek out this finality. Already in the series of *Cathedral of Rouen* one finds no concern for suggesting effects of mass, but only a desire to observe light

La Cathédrale de Rouen: Harmonie grise, temps gris.

in all of its intensities. It was mainly at Giverny, in the garden that he arranged himself, that Monet achieved his dream in a magic art free of any concern for stable form. His garlands of wisterias, reflected in the shifting mirror of the lake, his sheets of water lilies floating on the changing water, provided him with a whole dazzling play of colored mirages that were their own justification, like certain variations in music whose theme is nothing more than a pretext and a place to start.

The whole development of Monet's work was toward a complete liberation that allowed him, near the end of his life, to arrive at an art as independent of reality as that of the most abstract painters of today. The astonishing mural ensemble inspired by *Water Lilies*, demonstrates the attainment of a poetical world rid of all concern with form, a world in which the evocation of reality is no more than a vague pretext. A curious magic emanates from it, but

The Bridge.

St. Lazare Station: The Arrival of the Train from Normandy.

Water Lily Pond.

The Japanese Footbridge.

The Garden at Giverny.

The Bridge at Argenteuil.

also the certainty that a point has been reached that cannot be passed, a point where the artist, at the height of his powers has discovered a purity beyond which he cannot go without dissolution.

This extreme experiment could not have been attained if Monet had not previously undertaken many times to paint the same landscape seen at different hours, in different seasons, under different lights, with the sole purpose of extracting new effects from the same subject. The views of *The Gare Saint-Lazare* (1876-1877), of *Rouen Cathedral* (1892-1894) and of the garden at Giverny (1905-1908) are among the most celebrated, but there are

other sequences, *The Ice Breaking* (1880), *Haystacks* (1891), *Poplars on the Banks of the Epte,* and the views of London and Venice, that deserve being equally known.

Those fortunate enough to have seen several canvases on the same theme, assembled and exhibited by the artist at the Durand-Ruel Gallery, realized the interest and appeal of such a grouping. In them Monet demonstrated that no absolute color exists in Nature, only light; and that since the appearance of all objects changes perpetually, the art of the painter should consist in choosing one moment in preference to any other, in order to fix its individuality in a definitive image. The demonstration is convincing,

Terrace at Ste.-Adresse.

The Artist's Garden at Vétheuil. ➤

although Impressionism would have been justified even without it.

It is easy to understand why this art, which at the beginning won the support and encouragement of Naturalists in literature, who regarded it as an illustration of their theories of objective reality, was later disowned by the same writers. It was, in fact, not so much a Naturalist expression that Monet sought as a poetry of suggestions in which imprecision and the absence of clear figures leave a large place for dreaming and a constantly renewed play of color.

Monet's art, as it appears to us today, claims no ancestry in the past, even though some of the painters of the eighteenth century seem to have been its forerunners. The art of Monet, in fact, remains closer to Nature; and if a

divergence seems occasionally to exist, the explanation is that the painter's eye has succeeded in catching what previously seemed impossible to seize. He is quite distinct from some of the other painters classified as Impressionists. He has almost nothing in common with the rigorous draftsmanship of Degas, except when Degas, in later years, indulged, in his pastels and particularly for his dancers, in similar iridescences; his construction was entirely different from Cézanne's, and he had real kinship only with Sisley and Pissarro, although he has more assurance than they. Jongkind and Boudin paved the way for him and succeeded in transcribing similar wet atmospheres in their own manner, but without achieving the poetical quality that remains the unique achievement of Monet.

← ← *Woman with a Parasol: Madame Monet and Her Son.*

Boulevard des Capucines. →

← *Rue Montorgueil.*

Charing Cross Bridge.

*Poplars on the
Banks of the Epte.*